ALPENA COUNTY LIBRARY
211 N. First St.
Alpena, Mich. 49707

Gay and Lesbian Rights
A Struggle

Gay and Lesbian Rights

A Struggle

Marilyn Tower Oliver

Enslow Publishers, Inc.

40 Industrial Road   PO Box 38
Box 398   Aldershot
Berkeley Heights, NJ 07922   Hants GU12 6BP
USA   UK
http://www.enslow.com

To my cousin Terry Scott and his friend,
the late Timothy Heidel.

Library of Congress Cataloging-in-Publication Data

Oliver, Marilyn Tower.
   Gay and lesbian rights: a struggle / by Marilyn Tower Oliver.
      p. cm. —
   Includes bibliographical references and index.
   Summary: Examines the issue of gay and lesbian rights in the
United States, covering the history of the gay rights movement, the
current struggles it faces, and arguments both for and against it.
   ISBN 0-89490-958-4
   1. Gay rights—United States—Juvenile literature. 2. Gay
liberation movement—United States—Juvenile literature. [1.Gay
rights. 2. Gay liberation movement. 3. Homosexuality.] I. Title.
(Springfield, N.J.)
HQ76.8.U5055   1998
305.9'0664'0973—dc21   98-21258
                                       CIP
                                       AC

Illustration Credits: Jill Abrams, p. 72; Courtesy of Carl A.
Kroch Library, Cornell University, pp. 30, 63; Jackie Goldberg,
p. 46; Winn Krafton, pp. 36, 50, 57, 88; Courtesy of the
Library of Congress, pp. 24, 28, 32; The Names Project, p. 84;
National Gay and Lesbian Task Force, pp. 9, 12, 74; Marilyn
Tower Oliver, pp. 22, 41, 98; Lou Sheldon, pp. 101.

Cover Illustration: Winn Krafton.

Contents

Acknowledgments

The author wishes to thank the following organizations for their assistance: AIDS Project Los Angeles, American Civil Liberties Union, Family Research Council, Gay Men's Health Crisis, Lambda Legal Defense and Education Fund, National Gay and Lesbian Task Force, and Traditional Values Coalition.

The Fight for Gay Rights

Homosexuals are people who have a sexual preference for members of their own sex. The term *gay* refers to male homosexuals; female homosexuals are called lesbians. Throughout history gay men and lesbian women have faced prejudice because of their sexual orientation. The prejudice they have faced includes discrimination on the job, at school, in obtaining housing, and in the ability to function in society. At times, the prejudice has resulted in violence.

One day in May 1988, Rebecca Wight and Claudia Brenner were backpacking on

the Appalachian Trail in south central Pennsylvania. Claudia was thirty-one, and Rebecca was twenty-eight. Along the trail, they encountered a stranger who tried to involve them in conversation. Suddenly, the quiet of the afternoon was shattered by gunfire. Claudia was hit in the arm, neck, and face. Rebecca was struck in the back and head; the shot in her back exploded her liver and killed her. The stranger, Stephen Roy Carr, shot them because they were lesbians.[1]

William Hassel, a gay man who lived in Washington, D.C., was invited to a party by two young men. Instead of going to the party, they took him to a dark park where they forced him at knife point to take off his clothes. Then they beat him and kicked him, and they called him names such as "queer" and "faggot." One of the young men said he was going to kill Hassel. When the man swung the knife at his throat, Hassel grabbed it and then rolled his body into the assailant's legs, causing him to fall. Hassel was able to escape his captors and run away. The two young men were arrested, but in the trial that followed they were given light sentences of community service.[2]

Examples of physical and verbal abuse against homosexuals are not uncommon. The first national study of violence against gays and lesbians was made in 1984. Of the 2,074 individuals surveyed, 94 percent reported being spat upon, chased, hit, or assaulted with a weapon. Some had their property vandalized.[3] Since then, however, there has been

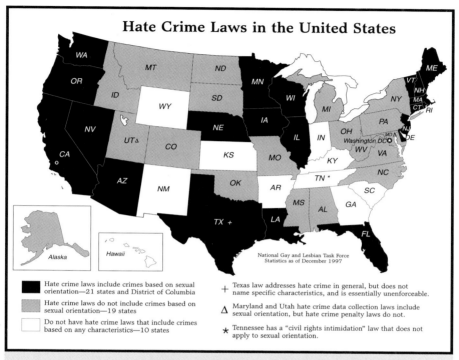

Hate Crime Laws in the United States

WA
MT
ND
ME
OR
MN
ID
SD
WI
VT
NH
WY
NY
MA
CT RI
NV
NE
IA
MI
PA
UTΔ
CO
IL
IN
OH
Washington DC
NJ
MD
DE
CA
KS
MO
WV
VA
AZ
NM
OK
AR
KY
NC
TN *
SC
MS
AL
GA
TX +
LA
FL

Alaska   Hawaii

National Gay and Lesbian Task Force
Statistics as of December 1997

■ Hate crime laws include crimes based on sexual orientation—21 states and District of Columbia

▨ Hate crime laws do not include crimes based on sexual orientation—19 states

□ Do not have hate crime laws that include crimes based on any characteristics—10 states

+ Texas law addresses hate crime in general, but does not name specific characteristics, and is essentially unenforceable.

Δ Maryland and Utah hate crime data collection laws include sexual orientation, but hate crime penalty laws do not.

★ Tennessee has a "civil rights intimidation" law that does not apply to sexual orientation.

As of December 1997, twenty-one states and the District of Columbia had hate crime laws that included violent crimes committed against people because of their sexual orientation.

growing activism on the part of gays and lesbians demanding that they be treated with equality.

In some cases, their protests have been very vocal. In September 1991, for instance, Governor Pete Wilson of California vetoed a bill passed by the legislature that would have forbidden job discrimination against gays and lesbians. The governor has the authority to reject laws that are passed by the state legislature. When news of the veto was released, the gay community was outraged. In his election campaign, Wilson had promised gay activists that he would support the bill. A spontaneous demonstration broke out on the streets of West Hollywood, a community in southern California with a large gay population. Approximately four hundred demonstrators marched that night. And every night for two weeks the demonstrations grew. Finally, the demonstrators went to the state capital in Sacramento, where several thousand men and women marched, shouting, "Gay rights now!"[4]

Gay and lesbian activists want acts of discrimination against homosexuals to be specifically forbidden by law in the United States. As of 1998, ten states had civil rights laws that included sexual orientation as a protected category. These states were California, Connecticut, Hawaii, Massachusetts, Minnesota, New Hampshire, New Jersey, Rhode Island, Vermont, and Wisconsin.[5]

Equal Protection Under the United States Constitution

In theory, the United States Constitution and the Bill of Rights guarantee equal protection against unfair treatment to everyone. In actual practice, however, some groups of citizens have been denied equal treatment. African Americans and other racial minorities have had to fight for the right to have equal access to housing, to attend the same schools as whites, to vote, and to be considered for employment. Women have also had to fight for equal treatment. Because these other groups have fought for their rights, federal and state laws now exist making it illegal to discriminate on the basis of race, sex, religion, handicaps, age, or national origin. Gay men and lesbian women believe that discrimination based on sexual orientation should also be illegal.

Those who oppose equal rights for gays and lesbians believe that homosexuality is an abnormal behavior. They point out that laws governing sexual behavior have existed in almost every society throughout the world.

Sodomy laws prohibit oral and anal sex, even between consenting adults. Most sodomy laws apply to both heterosexuals and homosexuals, but they are primarily used against lesbians and gay men to deny them other rights. The laws have been used to take children away from gay parents. And statutes in some cities have been used to arrest gay people for discussing sex. In states with sodomy laws, those found guilty may receive fines and jail time. Sodomy laws vary from state to state.

What Causes Homosexuality?

The majority of people are heterosexuals—people who are attracted to the opposite sex. No one knows exactly how large a percentage of the population is homosexual, but estimates run from 2 percent to 10 percent.

Although the causes of homosexuality have not been established, most homosexuals seem to have no choice in the matter of attraction. Some gay people

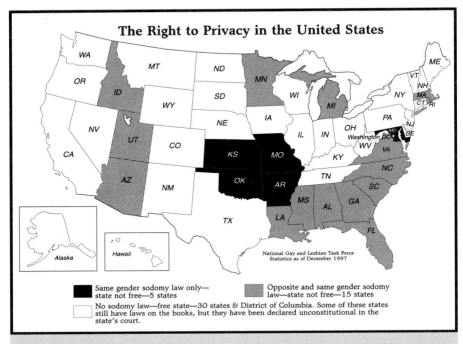

The Right to Privacy in the United States

National Gay and Lesbian Task Force
Statistics as of December 1997

Same gender sodomy law only—state not free—5 states

Opposite and same gender sodomy law—state not free—15 states

No sodomy law—free state—30 states & District of Columbia. Some of these states still have laws on the books, but they have been declared unconstitutional in the state's court.

As of December 1997, twenty states had laws forbidding sodomy between consenting adults.

say that they were aware of their attraction to others of the same sex at the age of four or five.[6]

The earliest studies of the causes of homosexuality focused on genetics. Genes are the biological building blocks that transmit characteristics such as eye color and height from parents to children. To try to prove that homosexuality is transmitted genetically, some researchers studied twins who shared the same environment and upbringing.

There are two kinds of twins: identical and

fraternal. Identical twins are created when the mother's fertilized ovum splits or divides into two fetuses (a fetus is an unborn baby). These twins share the same genetic makeup, and they are always of the same sex. Fraternal twins are created when the mother produces two ova that are fertilized separately. These twins have different genetic makeups. One study by Franz J. Kallmann, M.D., reported to the New York Neurological Society in 1951, indicated that when one identical twin male was homosexual, the other usually was too. Among the nonidentical twins studied, more than half of those with a homosexual brother were heterosexuals.[7]

Other researchers propose that homosexuality is caused by a hormonal difference between gays and nongays. Hormones are substances that stimulate body functions and behavior. Studies that have tried to prove this theory have not been successful. Gay men who were injected with testosterone, a male hormone, did not change their sexual orientation.

Some people believe that homosexuality is caused by the environment in which a child is raised. They suggest that a boy who has a strong mother and a weak or absent father is more likely to become gay than other boys. They also suggest that an early homosexual experience may cause a person to become gay.

Under some conditions, heterosexuals participate in homosexual activities. When people are forced to live in situations where there are no members of the opposite sex, their sexual outlets may involve homosexuality. This can occur in the military or in prison. Between 1979 and 1980, researchers Wayne S. Wooden and Jay Parker studied sexual behavior in a California medium security prison with a population of over twenty-five hundred men. The great majority of the inmates said they were heterosexual, but many had engaged in homosexual relations while in prison.[8]

Although the causes of homosexuality have not yet been firmly established, they are important in the discussion of gay rights. Many homosexuals argue that they should not be persecuted for something they cannot change. Many opponents of gay rights believe that homosexuals make a choice to live a gay lifestyle, which they believe is immoral. These opponents argue that granting equal rights to homosexuals threatens traditional values such as religion and the family.

2

The History of Homosexuality in Society

Homosexual behavior has always been a part of human existence. In the ancient world, the Greeks and Romans were tolerant toward homosexual behavior. Some artworks of the ancient Greeks portray homosexual acts, and some Greek writers wrote about homosexuality. The poet Sappho, one of the few female writers whose works have survived, praised love between two women. The word *lesbian* is derived from the island of Lesbos where Sappho was born.[1] In Rome, homosexuality was not considered illegal until the sixth century A.D., when it was outlawed by rulers who had converted to Christianity.[2]

The ancient Jews, or Hebrews, were a nomadic people who lived in the country that today is Israel. While the Romans and Greeks believed in many gods, the Jews worshiped one god. In Jewish scriptures, the books of Leviticus and Kings contain verses that forbid homosexual acts. These passages, along with sections of the New Testament, are still cited by religious groups as the basis for their opposition to gay rights legislation.

Christianity developed from the life and work of Jesus of Nazareth. The Christians along with the Jews believed that homosexuality was sinful.[3] Christian and Jewish viewpoints on homosexuality were strong forces in determining how gay people would be treated in the Western world from the Roman era to the present.

Homosexuality Was Scorned in Europe

After the Roman Empire was defeated by northern European tribes in the fifth century, Europe was dominated by the Catholic Church. In the thirteenth century Thomas Aquinas, a Catholic priest, condemned homosexuality as a vice against nature and a violation of the will of God.[4]

In 1562, English law made homosexual acts a crime for which a man could be punished by death. This law remained on the books for 266 years until it was finally repealed in 1828. During this period homosexuals could also be punished by being placed in the pillory, a cruel device made of wood with holes to secure the head and hands so that prisoners could not move. Sometimes street vendors sold rotten fruit and vegetables and the bodies of dead cats and dogs to onlookers as objects to throw at the prisoners. Because the prisoners were locked into the pillory, they could not protect themselves from being beaten.[5]

Even though homosexual acts were illegal, they continued to occur. In seventeenth-century England, some delinquent rich and aristocratic men, most of them heterosexuals, formed clubs that were infamous for behavior that included assault, rape, and drinking. One club, the Mollies, was made up of homosexuals. Inns that catered to male prostitutes were called Molly houses. By the eighteenth century, London had a subculture of such gay pickup points and houses of prostitution.[6]

Homosexuality in America

The early settlers believed that homosexuality was a terrible crime that should be punished by death. The earliest known incident of a gay man being put to death in America happened in St. Augustine, Florida, in 1566, when a Frenchman was executed by Spanish military authorities. Executions for homosexual acts also occurred in colonial Virginia, Connecticut, and New York.

Lesbians also received harsh treatment. In 1636 a proposal was made to the Massachusetts Bay Colony that women homosexuals receive the same punishment as men. In 1656, the New Haven

Colony in Connecticut passed a law requiring death for lesbianism as well as for male homosexuality.[7]

During the American Revolution there was a movement away from executions for those found guilty of homosexuality. Between 1777 and 1779, Thomas Jefferson and some other liberal reformers argued that the Virginia law should substitute castration for execution for those found guilty of homosexual acts.[8] Castration is the surgical removal of a man's testicles.

American Homosexuals in the Early Twentieth Century

Up to the early twentieth century, most homosexuals continued to keep their sexual orientation hidden because of the prejudice against them. Those who lived in small towns were particularly isolated. "I felt I was the only one until I left home," said one older man interviewed in the video *Before Stonewall: The Making of a Gay and Lesbian Community*. Home for this man was in North Carolina.[9]

In cities, some homosexuals interacted in an underground society. In the 1920s and 1930s, the speakeasy or nightclub was a place where many urban gays and lesbians gathered. A speakeasy was a bar where alcoholic drinks were sold during the era of Prohibition (1920–1933), a time when selling alcoholic beverages was against the law in the United States. In New York City, one openly lesbian bar owner, Gladys Bentley, dressed as a man in pants and tuxedos.

Many urban homosexuals lived a lifestyle that was separate and different from the rest of society, and they developed their own literature. In the 1920s, *The Well of Loneliness*, a novel by the lesbian British author Radclyffe Hall, became a best-seller. When the book was published in the United States in 1928, police seized more than eight hundred copies, stating that the book violated a law against circulating indecent literature. The censorship that surrounded the novel brought it more publicity and made it more famous.[10]

The censorship continued. After several plays dealing with homosexuality were produced in the 1920s, a law was passed in New York State making references to homosexuality in dramatic works illegal. In the 1930s, this censorship extended to movies. The Motion Picture Code of 1935 banned homosexuality in films.[11]

World War II

During World War II (1941–1945), as thousands of young men joined the armed forces, many homosexuals also enlisted or were drafted into military service. Many women, including lesbians, also signed up for military service. For many homosexuals from small towns, this was the first time that they had been in a setting where they could meet others who were gay. Gay bars became meeting places for homosexual servicepeople.

In the 1950s, homosexuals working in the government faced extreme prejudice. From 1950 to

1954, Senator Joseph McCarthy of Wisconsin conducted a nationwide campaign to expose communists in the government and in the arts. Homosexuals were thought to be security risks and were also targets of investigation. Discovery of homosexual activity was grounds for being fired from a government job.[12]

It took a great deal of courage for individuals to admit that they were gay or lesbian in the climate of the 1950s. Many homosexuals hid their sexual preference and attempted to blend into society. When they gathered in groups in bars or at parties, they were subject to police entrapment and arrest. Entrapment is tricking someone into committing an illegal act so that they can be arrested. In spite of the dangers, some individuals did band together to organize the first organizations for gays and lesbians in the United States.

The Mattachine Society

Fearing persecution, gays and lesbians were hesitant to form organizations to fight discrimination. But in 1925, Henry Gerber, a World War I veteran, formed the Society for Human Rights in Chicago, an organization that encouraged gays to get together to discuss society's attitude toward homosexuality. The members wanted to abolish the Illinois laws that criminalized homosexual acts. The organization was short-lived, however, because the organizers were arrested and charged with sending obscene literature through the mail.[13]

A more successful organization for gay males was founded in Los Angeles in 1950 by actor and activist Harry Hay and four of his friends. The organization was called the Mattachine Society, named after secret fraternities of unmarried townsmen in medieval France who were called *mattachines*. The *mattachines* dressed as women and wore masks when they performed in public. Hay said, "We took the name Mattachine because we felt that we 1950s gays were also a masked people."[14]

Soon after it was founded, the Mattachine Society was called upon to fight for the rights of one of its members. In 1952, Dale Jennings, one of the original members, was arrested by the Los Angeles vice squad. He was charged with indecent behavior. At that time, in order to make an arrest, undercover police officers would often try to trick gay men into soliciting homosexual acts. Many victims were afraid to fight charges stemming from such an arrest. Public exposure could mean humiliation, the disgrace of having a criminal record, and losing one's job. The Mattachine Society defended Jennings, who publicly admitted that he was gay although he said he was innocent of the charges against him. He was found not guilty and was freed.[15]

The Mattachine Society also fought censorship of gay-oriented literature. In 1954, the society went to court to fight the U.S. Post Office for the right to send *One Magazine* through the mail. The magazine, which had been started by the society, was the first publication for gays to be widely circulated in

Clinton comes to dinner, Sandra Bernhard, and Halloween pictures

FRONTIERS
N E W S   M A G A Z I N E

VOLUME 16
ISSUE 15

Hey Good Lookin',
What You Got
Cookin'?

Great Thanksgiving Recipes
How to pick the perfect wine
for every meal—even KFC
Brugge, Belgium: chocolate heaven
Plus, a special restaurant guide

NOVEMBER 28, 1997

Southern
California's
Gay Biweekly

COMPLIMENTARY

In 1954 the Mattachine Society went to court to fight a ban on sending gay publications through the mail. Today, publications about homosexuality, such as this magazine distributed in Los Angeles, are openly available to anyone.

America. The postal service in California refused to allow the magazine to be sent through the mail, saying it violated a law declaring the mention of homosexuality in print to be obscene. When a California court sided with the postal service, the publishers took the case to the United States Supreme Court, which ruled in their favor. This ruling established the legality of sending material about homosexuality through the mail.[16]

The rising popularity of inexpensive paperback books led to an increase in gay and lesbian literature. Much of this literature was controversial. Thousands of copies of *Howl*, a book of poetry by Allen Ginsberg, were seized by the police. The publicity surrounding the censorship of the book served to make it more visible, and soon it was America's best-selling book of poetry.[17]

Lesbians also wanted an organization where they could express their views. In 1955, a group of San Francisco women formed the Daughters of Bilitis, the first lesbian organization in the United States. The name was taken from a narrative by Pierre Louÿs about an ancient Greek lesbian poet who lived with Sappho on the island of Lesbos. The organization helped unite lesbians.[18]

Mental Health Decisions Change Opinions about Gays

Throughout history most of the prejudice against gays and lesbians has been based on the idea that their sexual practices were sinful. Before the

When poet Allen Ginsberg published Howl, *a book of poems, it was banned, but it soon became a best-seller.*

twentieth century, doctors tried to cure homosexuals with electroshock therapy, hypnosis, and treatments such as cold showers. In the early twentieth century, studies of human behavior looked for other explanations. Many psychiatrists believed that homosexuality was a mental disorder (psychiatrists are medical doctors who treat mental illness). They based their opinions on their experiences in therapy with homosexuals who were emotionally ill. Later findings, however, challenged this belief.

In 1948, zoologist Alfred Kinsey published the results of his studies on the sexuality of the human male in his book *Sexual Behavior in the Human Male*. His studies showed that 37 percent of adult men had experienced sex with another man at least once. Although many of these men were not gay, it appeared that homosexual behavior was not that unusual. Kinsey's research led him to believe that it was difficult, if not impossible, to define people in terms of their sexual behavior.[19] Although some experts today challenge his research techniques and say that the number of homosexuals is much lower than his estimate, Kinsey's studies caused many people to look seriously at the issue of sexual orientation.[20]

A few years after Kinsey's book was published, researchers Clellan S. Ford and Frank A. Beach published the results of their studies of seventy-six different cultures. The researchers found that in forty-nine of these cultures some homosexual behaviors were accepted. Their research on the sexual behavior of male monkeys also indicated that same-sex activity occurs in some animals. Their conclusion was that there is an inherent tendency for homosexuality in all animal species.[21]

The findings of Kinsey, Ford, and Beach undermined the argument that homosexuality was a mental illness.

During the mid-1950s, psychologist Evelyn Hooker's studies of homosexuals set the groundwork for a change in the way mental health professionals looked at homosexuality. Dr. Hooker administered identical psychological tests to both a group of homosexuals and a group of heterosexuals to see if the gay men had a greater occurrence of mental illness. Her studies showed that two thirds of each group had average or better-than-average mental health.

Because of the recognition given to Hooker for her studies she was named to head the National Institute of Mental Health's Task Force on Homosexuality in the late 1960s. The task force asserted that most of the problems experienced by homosexuals were the result of discrimination by society.

During the annual meeting of the American Psychiatric Association in 1972, a gay psychiatrist wearing a disguise and calling himself Dr. Anonymous addressed the group. He announced that there were over two hundred homosexual psychiatrists in attendance at the conference. Because homosexuality was considered an illness by the association, these doctors had to hide their sexual identities; they would meet secretly at the annual conventions.

The members of the American Psychiatric Association realized they needed to reevaluate their beliefs about homosexuality. At their annual convention in 1973 the psychiatrists voted to stop defining homosexuality as a mental illness. A statement was issued stating that "homosexuality . . . by itself does not necessarily constitute a psychiatric disorder."

The news of this decision made headline news in the major newspapers across the country. In their coverage of the historic decision, the gay newspaper *The Advocate* used the headline "Sick No More." Removing the shame of mental illness from homosexuality changed the way that gays and lesbians were viewed in much of society.[22]

Fighting for Gay Rights

The 1960s were a period of nonviolent protests against the war in Vietnam and against racism and discrimination in America. Gays and lesbians followed the example of African-American activists by demonstrating openly against the way they were being treated by society. Gay men and lesbians regularly marched in front of the White House, the Pentagon, and the State Department to protest the government's hiring and firing policies.[23] Picketing was not without its risks, though. It took a great deal of courage to protest because government agents took photos and wrote down names of the protesters.

The Stonewall Rebellion

Many homosexuals believe that the modern gay rights movement was born on the night of June 27, 1969, when the Stonewall Inn, a gay bar in New York City's Greenwich Village, was raided by police. Up to this time, most protests had been nonviolent. Gay bars were frequently the targets of police raids. In New York City there was a law that allowed police

Following the Stonewall Rebellion, more and more gays took to the streets to demand their rights.

to arrest and fine men found guilty of same-sex dancing, touching, and kissing.

On the night of June 27, the police entered the dimly lighted bar, switched on the lights, and began to force patrons into patrol cars. The night was warm, so there were many people milling about on the street outside the bar. Among them were many gays who shouted and jeered at the police officers. The jeers of the onlookers soon turned to violence. They began to throw bottles and trash at the officers, who retreated to the bar and called for reinforcements. The streets were cleared, but the anger remained. For the next two nights, crowds and riot police clashed in front of the Stonewall Inn. Trash cans were set on fire. The streets finally became quiet, but the feeling remained that homosexuals had finally stood up for their rights. The event gave many gays the courage to openly admit their homosexuality. Many became activists.[24]

Although the struggle to gain equal treatment would be difficult, some homosexuals began to meet with politicians to demand their rights. Some gays held "kiss-ins" at restaurants that had refused to serve them. Others applied for same-sex marriage licenses. At the Democratic National Convention held in Miami in 1972, two openly gay delegates addressed the convention in support of gay rights.[25]

In 1973, the National Gay and Lesbian Task Force was founded with the purpose of educating society to allow homosexuals to function to their full potential. The task force worked to have a gay rights bill introduced in the United States Congress. Congresswoman Bella Abzug of New York sponsored the bill (HR5242), which would have forbidden discrimination on the basis of sexual preference. Introduced in March 1975, the bill failed to pass, but it brought national attention to the issue of gay rights.[26]

Backlash

Not everyone was in favor of granting homosexuals protected civil rights status. Many people believed that homosexuality was immoral. Some Christians denounced homosexuality as a threat to the accepted concept of family relationships.

Among those who spearheaded the protests against gay rights during the 1970s was popular singer Anita Bryant. As spokesperson for the Florida juice industry, Bryant was a nationally visible figure. A strong opponent of gay rights, she organized the

In 1975, political activists Bella Abzug and Ed Koch of New York held a press conference to announce the first federal gay rights bill, introduced through the efforts of the National Gay and Lesbian Task Force.

Save Our Children crusade. The crusade gathered sixty-four thousand signatures on a petition to repeal a Dade County, Florida, law that banned discrimination based on sexual preference in housing, jobs, or public accommodations. Bryant also fought to ban gay teachers from schools because she believed they represented a moral and physical risk for children. Bryant's campaign became national.[27]

The Murder of Harvey Milk

In 1978, gays in San Francisco made a defiant show of strength by staging Gay Freedom Day. Three hundred seventy-five thousand people marched through the streets of the city. Harvey Milk, a gay candidate for city supervisor, urged them to be open about their homosexuality.

Milk won the election and was probably the first openly gay man to be elected to office in the United States. A short time after the election, however, Dan White, a former city supervisor, went to city hall and killed both Milk and Mayor George Moscone. Moscone, a heterosexual, had supported gay rights. White had been very outspoken against gay rights when he had been a supervisor.

Six months later a jury decided that White should serve only a six-year sentence for the murders. In response, angry gays marched to San Francisco's city hall. The demonstration turned into a riot, which was later called the White Night Riot. Dozens of policemen were injured trying to control the riot.[28]

For many years gay men and lesbians were afraid to admit their sexual orientation. In the 1970s, however, many took to the streets to protest, as in this 1976 march in San Francisco.

Since that time, many gays and lesbians have openly declared their homosexuality. Also, gays and lesbians have been elected to public offices in a number of communities.

Homosexuals have fought for the same rights guaranteed to all Americans by the United States Constitution. They want civil rights protection so that they can openly serve in the military, marry and raise children, and hold jobs without fear of being fired. There are still large numbers of people who do not believe that gays and lesbians deserve civil rights protection. They feel that open homosexuality is a threat to society and to the family.

3

Discrimination on the Job

One of the greatest concerns of gays and lesbians is that they may lose their jobs because someone in power disapproves of homosexuality. They also fear harassment on the job.

Virginia Uribe, a teacher who started a gay support group called Project 10 at Fairfax High School in Los Angeles, says that she receives five to ten calls a month from teachers in California who report harassment by students.[1]

During an earthquake drill at Crenshaw High School in south central Los Angeles, English teacher Martin

Bridge was escorting his class down a stairway. Some of the students started calling out, "faggot, faggot." Soon other students joined in, and the shouts echoed in the stairwell.

Shortly before this incident, Bridge had told a student that he was gay and the news had spread. Before long, students would open his door and disrupt his classroom, yelling slurs like "fag" and "faggot." Bridge had been a popular teacher with students. "They loved him. They really did adore him. They had a friend in him, and they found out he was gay and they turned on him," a fellow teacher said.

The Los Angeles Unified School District has a policy of nondiscrimination against gays. Support groups for gay students exist at half of the district's forty-nine high schools. June is designated as Gay and Lesbian Pride Month in the schools. Nevertheless, homosexual teachers may still face prejudice in the classroom. "We form our own little groups to pat each other on the back and say we're o.k. and network," Bridge said, "but the truth is, in the classroom, we're still scared to death of dealing with the homophobia."[2]

Gay employees in all sectors of the workforce have felt the brunt of other people's prejudice, fear, and dislike of homosexuality. Brian McNaught is a corporate consultant and educator who presents workshops to help business managers and employees deal with prejudice against homosexuals in the workplace. He says gay and lesbian employees are sometimes threatened by having hate mail sent to their homes or offices, by receiving threatening phone calls, or by having their names written in graffiti in office bathrooms. They may be the objects of antigay jokes. Offensive cartoons or articles might be taped on office filing cabinets. Coworkers may use offensive language in their presence. Some gay employees have even received death threats.[3]

Other problems are discrimination in hiring, promotion, and evaluation. In states that do not include homosexuality in their civil rights laws, employers who dislike gays and lesbians can fire them practically without penalty. Studies by the

The Los Angeles Unified School District has a policy of nondiscrimination against gay and lesbian teachers.

National Gay and Lesbian Task Force show that between 1980 and 1991 more than one out of every three gay persons surveyed had experienced job discrimination. Among the actions reported were dismissal, harassment, denial of promotion, negative performance reviews, violence, and being barred from a trade or profession. Many concealed their sexual orientation out of fear.[4]

A Long History of Job Discrimination

During the 1950s the United States government was open in its prejudice against gays. Government employees who were discovered to be homosexual were fired. Even those suspected of being homosexual could lose their jobs.

In the 1950s, Franklin Kameny, an astronomer with a Ph.D. from Harvard, publicly challenged the government's antigay policy. Kameny was fired from his position in the Army in 1957 because he was a homosexual. He appealed the decision but lost in both the federal courts and the Army's legal system. He then tried to appeal to the United States Supreme Court, but his request for a hearing was denied.

Kameny developed a strategy that influenced future gay activists. He urged other gays to push for their rights rather than limit themselves to educating the public. He made up the slogan "Gay Is Good."[5]

In 1975, the Civil Service Commission finally reversed its decision banning gays in the federal government. By the 1990s, a growing number of state governments had passed laws to outlaw job discrimination based on sexual orientation. Some states also had passed laws adding sexual orientation to the list of protected civil rights categories—race, gender, national origin, religion, age, and disability. By 1993, more than 70 million Americans were covered by these laws. Some private companies and corporations have antidiscrimination policies, others do not.

In 1991, management at the Cracker Barrel Old Country Store, Inc., a restaurant chain with nearly fourteen thousand employees in sixteen states, started a policy barring gay workers. Cheryl Summerville, a lesbian cook in a Georgia branch of the company, was fired even though she had received outstanding evaluations during her four years on the job. Summerville then joined the sit-ins that had been organized to protest the antigay policy at the Cracker Barrel restaurants. Soon, she began to get obscene phone calls, and a rabbit was hanged from her mailbox. "We didn't realize there was so much hate out there," she said.[6]

In 1993, social worker Jesse Shaw was fired from her job after she brought a picture of herself, her partner, and their two dogs to show her coworkers. Her place of employment did not discriminate, but the state of Mississippi, which ran the mental retardation center where she worked, did. A coworker complained, and Shaw lost her job. When Shaw went to the Equal Employment Opportunity Commission to complain, she was told that antigay discrimination was not forbidden by federal law.[7]

Gays as Volunteers

Even in states where nondiscrimination laws forbid firing employees because of their sexual orientation, private organizations can refuse to allow homosexuals to participate as volunteers. For instance, gays have often been banned from participation in volunteer jobs that involve working with young people. One organization that bars homosexuals from participation is the Boy Scouts of America.

Timothy Curran had been a member of the Boy Scouts, earning the high award of Eagle Scout. He received publicity when he took a male date to his senior prom, and he was later quoted in the news as being proud to be gay. A few months later, when he applied to be an assistant scoutmaster for a troop in his northern California community, his application was denied. He filed a lawsuit against the Scouts, *Timothy Curran* v. *Mt. Diablo Council Boy Scouts of America*.

In a two-to-one decision, the California State court of appeals held that a state law prohibiting job discrimination against homosexuals did not apply to the Boy Scouts of America, a private organization. The decision also said that the Scouts had the right to keep out a gay adult leader who openly displayed behavior that the organization wanted to discourage.[8]

The case, which began in 1981, was finally heard by the California Supreme Court in January 1998. The Lambda Legal Defense and Education Fund, a nonprofit public interest law firm that fights for the rights of homosexuals, represented Curran. They argued that the action of the Boy Scouts was in violation of a state law barring discrimination in employment on the basis of sexual orientation.[9]

In another similar case in 1997, the California Fourth District Court of Appeals ruled that the Boy Scouts of America had the right to fire Chuck Merino as a leader because he was gay. Merino, a police officer from El Cajon, a town near San Diego, had been a scout leader for four years. In response, gay organizations in San Diego demanded that the city evict the Boy Scouts from their headquarters in city-owned property. Also, the El Cajon and San Diego police departments cut their ties with the Scouts to show support for Merino. "The Boy Scouts need to learn to judge people as individuals, not put everyone in a group and make judgments about them," Merino said.

One of the judges who ruled against Merino said that the First Amendment to the United States Constitution protected the Boy Scouts' freedom of association. A spokesman for the Boy Scouts said that the group has a right to set and maintain leadership standards and that the leaders should reflect the values of the organization.[10] Merino appealed the lower court's ruling to the California Supreme Court in the case *Merino* v. *San Diego Council Boy Scouts of America*. But in March 1998, the court ruled in favor of the Boy Scouts.

Like the Boy Scouts, some religious groups disapprove of homosexuality. They argue that

Some religious denominations encourage gays and lesbians to become part of their congregations.

because churches are private, voluntary organizations, they should have the right to exclude an individual whose behavior is at odds with the moral codes of the denomination.

Some denominations may allow gays and lesbians to attend services, especially if they do not draw attention to themselves, but they ban admitted homosexuals from serving as priests or ministers. Other churches such as the Society of Friends, the Unitarian Universalists, and the United Church of Christ allow gays and lesbians to become ministers.

Gays and lesbians participate in many Jewish congregations. In 1987, the Union of American Hebrew Congregations in Los Angeles passed a resolution to include gay and lesbian members in its congregations. In 1989, the Reform Judaism movement extended its support to welcome gay couples into congregations. Beth Chayim Chadashim synagogue in Los Angeles has a majority of gay and lesbian members.[11]

Colorado's Amendment 2

In the 1990s, a number of communities faced attempts to deny or take away equal rights for gays and lesbians. Many of these attempts have focused on repealing state and local laws or policies that offered civil rights protection to homosexuals in the workplace. In Colorado, Idaho, and Oregon, and in cities such as Cincinnati, Tampa, and Portland, Maine, voters were asked to vote against gay rights.[12]

In the 1992 elections in Colorado, where gays

had pushed for antidiscrimination laws, a majority of voters approved Amendment 2 as an addition to the state constitution. The amendment was backed by Colorado for Family Values, a conservative Christian group.[13] Amendment 2 forbade government agencies from adopting policies offering civil rights protection to gays. The law said that homosexual orientation, behavior, or relationship could not be the basis for a claim of minority status or of discrimination. It overruled local laws protecting homosexuals in the workplace in the cities of Aspen, Denver, and Boulder.[14]

Gays claimed that the Colorado amendment attacked their constitutional guarantee of equal protection before the law. Gay and lesbian organizations across the United States called for a boycott of Colorado and Colorado-based businesses to protest Amendment 2.[15]

Court challenges to the new amendment took almost four years. In May 1996, in the case of *Romer* v. *Evans*, the United States Supreme Court struck down Amendment 2, ruling that hostility toward homosexuals was not an acceptable basis for discrimination against them.[16] In the historic decision, the justices wrote that Amendment 2 classified homosexuals in a way that made them unequal to everyone else.[17]

Oregon's Proposition 9

A similar antigay proposition called Ballot Measure 9 was placed on the Oregon ballot in 1992 by the

Oregon Citizen Alliance, a right-wing group. The proposition called for removing protections against discrimination in housing and employment for gays and lesbians. It would have forbidden lawmakers from expanding civil rights laws to protect homosexuals from discrimination. A proposed amendment to the state constitution would have declared homosexuality to be abnormal. Openly gay and lesbian professionals would have been prevented from receiving licenses. Pro-gay books would have been banned from the libraries, and teachers would have been required to describe homosexuality as wrong.

In 1992, before the election, violence against homosexuals in Oregon increased 22 percent. In Portland and Eugene, the offices of organizations fighting against the initiative were attacked. Portland's police chief, who had marched in the city's Gay Pride parades, received death threats.[18]

The homosexual community and its supporters mounted an active campaign to defeat the proposition. Gays and lesbians stated that they only wanted to have the right to live their lives without discrimination. They were supported by most of the state's politicians and by business leaders who feared that passing the initiative would keep companies from locating in Oregon.

Supporters of the initiative argued that they didn't want gays to become visible in society. They believed that homosexuality was sinful behavior.

At the election, the proposition was defeated by

voters, although almost five hundred thousand voted in favor of restricting gay rights.[19]

What Do Gay Employees Want?

Brian McNaught says that gays and lesbians want companies and schools to ensure a level playing field so that all employees, gay or straight, have equal treatment and equal opportunities to advance. He says that worker efficiency is lowered when an employee is afraid to be honest about his or her sexual orientation.

Gay and lesbian employees want to be open about their relationships. They want to be able to include their partners in benefits such as health care. They also want to be able to place a picture of their partners on their desks and bring their partners to company social events. They want heterosexual coworkers to refrain from telling antigay jokes. McNaught said that in one survey of homosexuals, 90 percent said they had been present when an antigay joke had been told at work.[20]

Signs of Improvement

There are some signs indicating that homosexuals are becoming more accepted in the workplace. Many of the largest companies in the United States have nondiscrimination policies to protect gay employees on the job. Among these are General Motors, AT&T, IBM, Miller Brewing Company, Eastman Kodak, J.C. Penney, Sears, Roebuck & Co., and United Airlines. Some of these companies offer workshops where

Los Angeles councilperson Jackie Goldberg is one of many gay and lesbian legislators in the United States.

employees can discuss sexual diversity and discrimination.[21]

Some communities also offer health care benefits and funeral leave to their gay employees' domestic partners. Among these communities are Berkeley, West Hollywood, Los Angeles, and Santa Cruz, California; New York City; and Seattle.

A number of openly gay men and women now hold political offices. In 1996, there were four openly gay men serving in the United States Congress. They were Massachusetts Democrats Gerry Studds and Barney Frank, and Republicans Steve Gunderson of Wisconsin and Jim Kolbe of Arizona.[22] Los Angeles councilperson Jackie Goldberg is a lesbian, as is California assembly-person Sheila Keihl.

4

Lesbian and Gay Issues at School

Many of the same issues that adults face at work, homosexual students face at school. Gay students often experience harassment and name-calling by other students. Sometimes they experience violence. For a gay student, such memorable events as going to the senior prom may be forbidden by authorities. In recent years, however, some homosexual students have successfully fought the system.

Two California girls, Vanessa Alcazar and her date, Anna Gallegos, bought tickets to Vanessa's high school prom in anticipation of a memory-filled night. Four days before the prom, the school principal told the girls they could not attend. The girls decided to challenge his decision by going public on national television. Fellow students circulated a petition asking the principal to change his mind. Gloria Allred, a prominent attorney, took their case. She called the principal and threatened to bring a discrimination suit against the school district if he did not change his mind. Fifteen minutes after the call, he decided the girls could attend the dance.

Vanessa stated, "If you're gay, you should just be honest about it. There's no law that says we can't go together, and we have our rights just like straight people do."[1]

As gay and lesbian high school students have become more open about their sexual orientation, they have tried to form clubs and support groups where they can make friends with others like themselves. Some school districts have encouraged these clubs. Others have tried to forbid the clubs or have made it difficult for students to join.

In the spring of 1996, gay and lesbian students and their supporters in Glendale, California, convinced the board of education to drop a plan that would have required parents' permission for high school students to join campus clubs. The plan would have forced homosexual students to tell their parents about their sexual orientation in order to join a gay support club. One girl who spoke before the board said that she had to leave home after her parents found out that she was a lesbian.[2]

In Los Angeles, many gay and lesbian educators are open about their sexual orientation.

In some schools, groups of students have tried to block homosexual youths from participation in school activities, such as student government. In 1993, the student council at Bremerton High School in Washington State tried to amend the school constitution to ban openly gay students from holding school offices. A majority of the student body disagreed. The proposal was voted down by the general student body in a vote of 635 to 475.[3]

Schools Become a Battleground for Gay Rights

In the 1990s, the question of how homosexuality should be handled in the school setting became a matter of debate in many school districts. Some situations ended up as court cases. Others resulted in demonstrations.

In July 1996, the school board in Merrimack, New Hampshire, voted to bar education or counseling that encouraged students to treat homosexuality as a positive lifestyle. Parents and teachers sued the district over this policy. The lawsuit in the United States district court in Concord charged that the policy violated teachers' rights to free expression, guaranteed by the First Amendment to the United States Constitution.[4]

In February 1996, the school board in Salt Lake City, Utah, banned all extracurricular clubs rather than allow a group of gay students to form a support group at a local high school.[5] The board based its decision on a 1994 federal law that barred school districts from excluding student groups, such as religious clubs, from high school campuses. The law was the result of a court case, *Westside Community Board of Education* v. *Mergens*, that began in Nebraska in 1985. The case involved Bridget Mergens, a student in Omaha, Nebraska, who filed a lawsuit against the school district because it prohibited her from holding Bible club meetings at school. When the case reached the Supreme Court in 1990, the school district lost. The Court ruled that a school cannot discriminate against student clubs "on the basis of the religious, political, philosophical, or other content of the speech at such meetings."[6] This means that a school district cannot keep one group of students from forming a club when other school clubs exist.[7]

In Salt Lake City, after the school board ruled against the gay students, hundreds of students walked out of class and marched to the state capitol as a protest.[8]

Some people are afraid that acceptance of gay students is a threat to traditional values of marriage and family. They fear that presenting homosexuality as an alternative lifestyle encourages students to experiment in what is viewed by some as abnormal behavior. "I don't believe our young people should be placed in a position to deal with these kinds of issues," one man said in Salt Lake City.[9]

Gay activists and their supporters believe that all students have a constitutional right to equal treatment at school. Gay and lesbian students face problems of acceptance. They are often discriminated against, harassed, and even physically harmed. Many are afraid to tell their parents how they feel. Sometimes, a gay youth's feelings of separation have tragic consequences.

Gay Teens and Suicide

Many teenagers don't know how to deal with their feelings of homosexuality in a society that rejects gays. Friends and parents may be openly hostile; other students may make fun of them.

Bobby Griffith was a young man who couldn't deal with his homosexuality. Two months after his twentieth birthday he jumped off a freeway overpass and was instantly killed by a truck. He had grown up in a family that had told him homosexuality was sinful and gays would go to hell.

Many people believe that special programs for homosexual youths are necessary because gay teenagers commit suicide more often than heterosexual teens do. Statistics show that around 50 percent of gay teens think about or attempt suicide. Gay and lesbian youths account for 30 percent of teen suicides. Approximately fifteen hundred homosexual kids kill themselves every year.[10]

In 1989, a study on gay and lesbian teen suicide was conducted by the federal Department of Health and Human Services. The study found that homosexual teens were two to three times more likely to attempt suicide than were heterosexual youths.[11]

Not everyone accepts these statistics. Conservative groups such as the Washington, D.C.–based Concerned Women for America say that the report has errors. They believe that the 1989 study failed to look at other psychological factors, such as family problems and abuse, that might cause a young person to consider suicide.[12]

Many school districts do acknowledge that gay and lesbian teens have special problems. A number of programs have been set up to help them.

Providing a Safe Place for Gay and Lesbian Students

Many gay and lesbian students are harassed at school. They may be called names, or be physically attacked by other students, or even be murdered. Even some teachers make fun of them.

At the Harvey Milk School in San Francisco, the student body is made up mostly of gay students who have been bothered at other schools. The school is named after the gay city supervisor who was assassinated in 1978. More than 58 percent of the school's students say they were beaten up in their prior schools and were afraid they might not be able to finish their educations there.[13]

In Los Angeles, Project 10 was started by Virginia Uribe in 1984. Uribe, a lesbian teacher, started the program as a response to an incident in which a seventeen-year-old boy was bullied and harassed to the point of quitting school. When he told his parents that he was gay, they threw him out of the house. Uribe began a lunchtime discussion group with gay and lesbian students. Soon, the lunchtime group began to grow. She currently runs rap groups and trains teachers in skills to work with homosexual students. The Project 10 program is now in many Los Angeles city high schools.[14]

New York City's Hetrick-Martin Institute offers counseling, HIV/AIDS education, and a drop-in center where kids can get together after school. The institute was founded in 1979 after a boy was thrown out of a homeless shelter. When he was raped in the shelter, authorities there said he had invited the attack by being gay.

Both Project 10 and the Hetrick-Martin Institute offer gay and lesbian youths a place where they can talk with others who experience the same problems, such as lack of parent support and harassment by heterosexual students. Communication helps them break their feelings of isolation. These projects are most often found in large cities like New York City, Los Angeles, and San Francisco. Some young homosexuals leave hostile home situations and come to these larger communities in search of acceptance.[15]

Arguments Against Special Programs for Gay and Lesbian Students

Some opponents to special programs for gay and lesbian students believe that such programs promote homosexuality as a normal activity. They believe that presenting homosexuality as an alternative lifestyle implies that it is just another choice that a person can make. Groups such as the Traditional Values Coalition say that gay support programs fail to point out the negatives of homosexuality, which include a higher rate of sexually transmitted diseases, such as syphilis, genital warts, and AIDS. The coalition also objects to the fact that parents are not informed about the content of what is being taught in some programs. Some critics also believe that teaching students that 10 percent of the population is homosexually oriented is wrong. They point to other studies that place the figure between 2 percent and 4 percent of the population.[16]

Arguments in Favor of Special Programs for Gay Youths

Those who favor having gay and lesbian clubs and support groups at school believe that they are necessary to counter the prejudice that some gay youths have experienced starting as early as elementary school. There have been many instances where young gays and lesbians have experienced extreme intolerance.

By the time Jamie S. Nabozny was eleven, he knew he was gay. He tried to keep his sexual identity a secret from his classmates in the small town in Wisconsin where he lived. Nevertheless, they discovered his secret. When Jamie was in the seventh grade, two boys wrestled him to the ground and pretended to rape him. When he was in the ninth grade, schoolmates beat him and urinated on him in the boys' restroom. Even though he started going to school earlier and earlier to avoid being picked on, his tormentors still were determined to hurt him. One day when he was sitting outside the school library, ten boys came up to him. One kicked Jamie's books out of his hands. When he reached down to pick them up, the boy started to kick him. Jamie blacked out and eventually ended up in the hospital, where it was determined that he had internal bleeding and bruising.

Jamie Nabozny said that school districts did little to help him, even when his parents complained. "My middle school principal told me that if I was going to be openly gay, I had to expect this," he said. "In high

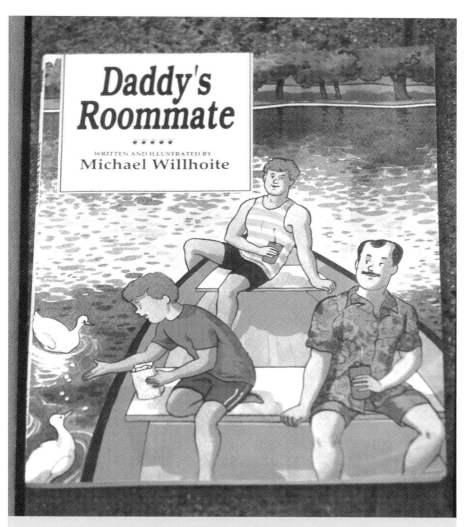

The children's book, Daddy's Roommate, *tries to explain same-sex relationships.*

school I was just kind of pushed out of the [school] office."[17] So Jamie decided to sue his high school.[18]

In a landmark ruling, the United States court of appeals said that the Equal Protection Clause of the Fourteenth Amendment to the United States Constitution required the state and the school to treat each person with equal regard. The ruling said that there was no rational reason for allowing one student to attack another based on the victim's sexual orientation.[19]

In November 1996, the Wisconsin school district agreed to pay Jamie almost $1 million. He received $900,000 and up to $62,000 for possible medical expenses for the injuries he received while he was a student.

"I'm very glad that the truth came out. Now, I can go on with my life. I feel like I have justice, and this means justice for other kids out there who aren't sure if they should stay in school or stay alive," Jamie said.[20]

5

Gays and Lesbians in the Military

Homosexuals have always served in the ranks of the army and navy. Most of the time they kept their homosexuality hidden because the military of the United States has had a strict policy of punishing anyone discovered to be a homosexual. Men and women who were discovered to be gay received dishonorable discharges and were denied their veterans' rights.

In the twentieth century, prohibitions against homosexuality became part of military law. During World War I (1914–1918), the act of sodomy was written into the Articles of War of 1916 as a felony crime. The Articles of War were military laws. Although sodomy (defined by the articles as an act of oral or anal sex) technically applied to both heterosexuals and homosexuals, most of the time the law was used to prohibit these acts by homosexuals. Through the 1920s and 1930s, homosexuality was treated as a crime. During this time, many gay soldiers and sailors were sent to prison.[1]

During World War II hundreds of gay men were among the millions who enlisted or were drafted. A number of lesbians also enlisted to help the war effort. They served in secret because military officials believed that homosexuals were not fit to serve. The officials feared that gays would undermine morale in the close living quarters on ships and in barracks, affecting military readiness. A psychological exam to screen out homosexuals was given to new recruits. Gays had to decide whether to lie and pass as heterosexuals or be sent home in disgrace.

Sexual acts between males were considered serious crimes that could be punished by a court-martial and hard labor in prison for as long as five years. Lesbians were removed from the military by being classified as mentally ill and, therefore, unfit to serve. When homosexuals were dismissed, they received a blue discharge called a Section 8, which meant that the person had undesirable character traits.[2]

Challenging the System

After the Stonewall Riots in 1969, when many gays took to the streets to openly demonstrate against discrimination, some military personnel who were accused of homosexuality began to fight back rather than accept prison sentences and dishonorable discharges.

In 1975, Technical Sergeant Leonard Matlovich decided to challenge the military's policy on gays. He wanted to test both the army's ban on homosexuals and the public's acceptance of gays. Matlovich, who had been awarded many medals for his service, told his commanders in the Air Force that he was gay. Matlovich had served in Vietnam and had received the Bronze Star for distinguished service, a Purple Heart because he had been wounded, and two Air Force Commendation medals. In all, he had served for eleven years.

On March 6, 1975, he wrote a letter to the Secretary of the Air Force. He closed with the words, "I consider myself to be a homosexual and fully qualified for further military service."[3]

On May 20, however, he received a letter stating that the military was starting actions against him to force his discharge.

Matlovich decided to fight the action. He received many offers to speak, and his photo appeared on the cover of *Time* magazine. In spite of his record of service, though, Matlovich was discharged as unfit for military service.[4]

Around the same time, Ensign Vernon Berg III, a young officer and graduate of the Naval Academy, was accused of homosexual behavior. Berg decided to challenge the Navy's policy on homosexuals by demanding a hearing. He hoped the Navy would reinstate him as an officer. The result of the hearing was that he was forced to leave the Navy.[5] In the end, both Matlovich and Berg had their discharges upgraded to honorable. But both men continued to fight their dismissals from the armed forces.

Although there is no specific guarantee of privacy in the United States Constitution, the right to be left alone is protected by the Fourth, Fifth, Ninth, and Fourteenth Amendments and has also been upheld in many Supreme Court decisions.[6] Matlovich believed that his discharge violated his constitutional rights to privacy and equal protection before the law. He wanted the Air Force to let him return to service. He decided to take his case to federal court, where it went before Judge Gerhard Gesell. The judge was sympathetic. Although he did not reinstate Matlovich, he did ask that the armed forces reexamine the policy against homosexuals.[7]

Matlovich decided to appeal. Ultimately, his case and that of Berg were joined into one case. On December 6, 1978, the United States court of appeals ruled that both men's discharges were illegal. The court said the military was unclear in the reasons that some homosexuals were allowed to remain in service while others like Matlovich and Berg were forced out. In effect, the court's ruling required the military to explain its reasons for its policies regarding homosexuals. The cases against the two men were sent back to the federal court.

In 1980, Judge Gesell ordered that Matlovich be

In 1975, Air Force Technical Sergeant Leonard Matlovich challenged the military policy against gays and lesbians. Matlovich, a highly decorated soldier, was discharged as unfit for military service.

reinstated into the Air Force at the rank he would have had if he had never been dismissed and that he be given back pay. Berg was also to be reinstated. Neither man chose to return to the military, but both accepted cash settlements. The decision paved the way for others to challenge the military's ban on gays. In the next two decades, many men and women would fight their discharges.[8]

Colonel Margarethe Cammermeyer

Lesbians have also been discharged from the military for their sexual orientation. Like Leonard Matlovich, Margarethe Cammermeyer had a distinguished military career. She joined the Army in 1961 and volunteered for duty in Vietnam, where she was a nurse during some of the most intense battles of the war. She was one of the few women to be awarded the Bronze Star for distinguished service. She also received a Meritorious Service Medal and two Army Achievement medals. After she left active service, Cammermeyer joined the Army Reserves, where she was selected Nurse of the Year in 1985.

Although Cammermeyer had been married and was the mother of four sons, she also knew she was a lesbian. After her divorce she stayed in the Army Reserves, achieving the rank of full colonel. She was chosen to be chief nurse of the Washington State National Guard. In 1987, she found out that she was being considered for the job of chief nurse for the National Guard of the United States. As a candidate for this position she was required to pass a security clearance. She vowed to herself that she would tell the truth about her sexuality if she were asked. When she was asked whether she was a homosexual, she answered, Yes.

The Army began proceedings to take away her rank in the Washington National Guard and discharge her from service. Many officials came to her defense, including the governor of Washington, but the military would not back down. In 1992, she was forced out of the military, which said that her same-sex attraction was harmful to her military service.

Cammermeyer decided to fight with the assistance of the Lambda Legal Defense and Education Fund. Her case went to federal court.[9] Cammermeyer was the highest ranking military officer to challenge the armed forces. In 1994, United States District Judge Thomas Zilly ruled in Cammermeyer's favor. "Prejudice, whether founded on unsubstantiated fears, cultural myths, stereotypes or erroneous assumptions, cannot be the basis for a discriminatory classification," Zilly wrote in his ruling.[10]

Don't Ask, Don't Tell

In 1993, President Bill Clinton came into office committed to lifting the ban on gays in the military. Congress and the Pentagon disagreed with the president. Enlisted men at some military bases called senators and congressmen to express their opinion that homosexuals were unfit for military service and would undermine morale.

In 1994, a new policy called Don't Ask, Don't Tell was put into effect. The rule was a compromise between President Clinton and the military and political leaders who opposed lifting the ban against homosexuals in the military. The policy was defined in the 1993 National Defense Authorization Act, the military's 1993–1994 budget, which was passed by Congress on November 17, 1993. The policy stated that the presence of openly gay and lesbian personnel was dangerous to military morale and discipline. It placed the military's antigay discrimination into federal law.[11] This new law allowed homosexuals to serve if they did not have sex with other service members and if they kept their sexual orientation and conduct private. Under this rule, a recruit was not asked about his or her sexual orientation. Gays and lesbians were expected to keep their homosexuality secret. Those who were openly gay or who were caught in homosexual acts could still be punished by discharge.

A study by the Servicemembers Legal Defense Network (SLDN) released in 1996 revealed that the military discharged 722 members for homosexuality in 1995. The SLDN said that 363 of these cases violated the Don't Ask, Don't Tell policy.[12] Another report released in 1998 revealed that 563 violations of the policy occurred in 1997.[13]

David Hackworth, a highly decorated soldier who served in the U.S. Army during the Korean and

Vietnam wars, expressed fears that openly gay soldiers would harm the troop morale necessary in combat. "On the battlefield what allows men to survive is combat units made up of disciplined team players, who are realistically trained and led by caring skippers who set the example and know their trade," he said.[14]

Eric Konigsberg, a reporter for the magazine *New Republic*, believes that gays and lesbians will not harm military morale. He points to the fact that homosexuals serve without problems in the armies of Holland, Denmark, Sweden, and Israel. A soldier in the Israeli Army said, "There were openly gay soldiers I encountered, but no one seemed to resent it. It's not even an issue."[15] In 1993, the Rand Corporation, a California research organization, reported that sexual orientation should not be relevant to military service. Rand researchers had visited seven foreign countries where gays successfully serve in the military.[16] The research noted that an emphasis on professional conduct and discipline was key to dealing with issues of privacy.[17]

A Challenge to the Ban

The Lambda Legal Defense and Education Fund argues that requiring lesbians and gay men to hide their homosexuality in order to serve in the military asks them to accept a judgment that their sexual orientation is disgraceful. In his July 1997 ruling in the case *Able* v. *Perry*, District Judge Eugene H. Nickerson rejected the Don't Ask, Don't Tell policy on constitutional grounds. Six gay and lesbian defendants argued that the law violated their constitutional rights of free speech and free expression protected by the First Amendment. They also argued that the law took away their right to equal protection because it intentionally discriminated against homosexual service members and treated them differently from others in the military.[18]

In his ruling Judge Nickerson wrote, "It is hard to imagine why the mere holding of hands off base and in private is dangerous to the mission of the Armed Forces if done by homosexuals, but not if done by a heterosexual."[19]

Matt Coles, director of the American Civil Liberties Union's Lesbian and Gay Rights Project said that the issue was one of equal treatment for everybody. "The military's ban on gay troops will eventually fall. It doesn't make sense to discharge able-bodied service members simply for their sexual orientation."[20]

6

Same-Sex Marriage and Gay Parents

The rights of same-sex couples to marry and the rights of gays as adoptive parents are two of the most controversial issues of the 1990s. Gays and lesbians have been the focus of debate as they challenge the definition of the traditional family. Although in the past homosexual parents often hid their sexual orientation, during the 1990s many have decided to openly acknowledge their identity. Although no one knows how many same-sex couples with children exist, researchers believe that the number is growing. Some researchers estimate that there could be as many as 16 million children who have at least one gay parent. Adoption agencies also report that there is a growing number of requests from gay and lesbian couples.[1]

Lily, a little girl from Tennessee, lives in a family with two mothers, both of whom are lesbians. Lily's biological father was a gay lawyer who donated his sperm, but he has no legal or financial obligation to help raise her. Lily's parents, an attorney and a drug- and alcohol-abuse counselor, are open about their relationship.[2]

A more high-profile couple, rock star Melissa Etheridge and her partner Julie Cypher, also decided to have a baby. Etheridge, who disclosed that she was a lesbian in January 1993, and Cypher had been together for eight years when they made their decision to start a family. Etheridge said, "I always wanted children in my life."[3]

Homosexual couples also want the respect and benefits that heterosexual couples enjoy through marriage. Advocates for gay rights believe that the decision to get married belongs to individuals, not to the state. Depriving gays and lesbians of the right to get married denies them their civil and human rights. Andrew Sullivan, former editor of *New Republic* magazine, wrote that being able to marry whomever one wishes is guaranteed in the Declaration of Independence's clause regarding the right to life, liberty, and the pursuit of happiness.[4] Groups fighting for equal rights for homosexuals, such as the Human Rights Campaign, the National

Gay and Lesbian Task Force, and the Lambda Legal Defense and Education Fund, believe that marriage is an important personal decision that should not be dictated by government.

Rights Denied to Same-Sex Couples

Because the committed relationships between homosexuals are not recognized under the law, gays and lesbians are sometimes denied the right to visit a sick or injured partner in the hospital.[5] Activists point to the case of Karen Thompson and Sharon Kowalski as an example of a couple whose rights were violated because their relationship was not legally recognized. The two lesbians shared a home in Minnesota and had exchanged rings. When Sharon was badly injured in an automobile accident, the hospital refused to let Karen visit her. Karen was denied any information about Sharon's condition and did not know whether she was dead or alive. Sharon Kowalski had a serious brain injury that required constant care. Karen Thompson had to spend more than three hundred thousand dollars and nine and a half years in an expensive court battle to win the right to visit and care for her spouse.[6]

Legalizing marriage for homosexuals is also a way for them to obtain benefits that married couples enjoy. These include health insurance, pension plans, and inheritance rights.[7] Married couples can keep a jointly owned home if one partner goes on Medicaid, dies, or becomes ill. A married person also can receive sick leave to care for an ailing spouse. A

Jill Abrams, a lesbian, designed a billboard that supports legalizing marriage for same-sex couples.

married person is also eligible for pensions and social security benefits after his or her spouse dies. Couples can file joint tax returns, which may save money.[8]

Since the late 1980s homosexuals have fought to obtain formal recognition of their relationships. At the 1993 March on Washington for Lesbian, Gay, and Bisexual Equal Rights and Liberation, same-sex marriage was high on the list of demands.

Domestic Partnerships

Domestic partnerships are another way for unmarried couples to enjoy the same benefits that married couples receive. Domestic partners are individuals who live together in a committed relationship without being legally married. These relationships allow partners to be listed on health insurance policies, life insurance policies, and pensions.

As a result of gay activism, some corporations and communities now recognize relationships between gays and lesbians and other unmarried couples and offer them the same benefits they provide to married employees. Some of the cities that offer such benefits are Madison, Wisconsin, Tacoma Park, Maryland, and New York City. As of 1995, approximately seventy-five private companies and organizations and many unions recognized domestic partners in member and employee health plans.[9]

Opponents of granting domestic partnership benefits say that society does not profit from these relationships. The benefits are very expensive, critics say. In 1997, the Los Angeles Unified School District was criticized by some citizens for a proposal to provide domestic partnership benefits to employees at an estimated cost of $4 million. Critics said this money could be better spent on classroom and education expenses.[10]

Those who support domestic partnership benefits say that they give same-sex partners the same protections that have been enjoyed by married heterosexuals for years. They believe that domestic partnership laws help bring greater social acceptance to gays and lesbian couples.[11]

They also point to the fact that benefits, such as life and health insurance, a pension, and profit-sharing, represent about 40 percent of a worker's actual income.[12]

Even though same-sex marriages have not been legally recognized, some gay couples have been able to publicly acknowledge their relationships in commitment ceremonies at their church or temple. These ceremonies are similar to marriage ceremonies, but because same-sex marriages are illegal in all states they do not carry the weight of the law. Although couples consider these committed relationships to be like a marriage, many homosexuals are not satisfied.

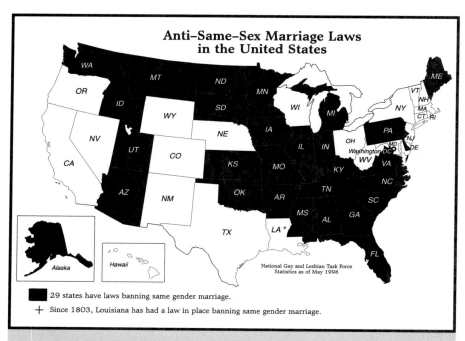

Anti–Same–Sex Marriage Laws in the United States

National Gay and Lesbian Task Force Statistics as of May 1998

■ 29 states have laws banning same gender marriage.

✛ Since 1803, Louisiana has had a law in place banning same gender marriage.

As of April 1998, marriage of same-sex couples was still prohibited in the United States. The Defense of Marriage Act, passed by congress in 1996 and signed by President Clinton, limited the definition of marriage to exclude same-sex couples.

They believe that, like heterosexuals, they should have the right to be legally married.

In the early 1990s, gays and lesbians began challenging the laws that said a marriage could only take place between a man and a woman. The first major challenge occurred in Hawaii.

Hawaii Tests the Law on Marriage

In 1990, three couples applied for marriage licenses in Honolulu. When they stepped up to the counter at the Department of Health to apply for licenses, their applications were denied. The couples decided to appeal their cases to the Hawaii Supreme Court. In 1993, the justices of that court ruled that denying same-sex couples the right to get married violated the equal protection clause in the state constitution unless there was a good reason for the discrimination. The case was known as *Baehr* v. *Miike*. (Ninia Baehr was one of the lesbians applying for a license. Lawrence Miike was the state health director.)

The case went to the circuit court for trial. At that trial in 1996, Circuit Court Judge Kevin S.C. Chang ruled that banning same-sex marriages is a form of discrimination. Hawaii thus became the first state to lift the ban on homosexual marriages.[13] In his ruling, Judge Chang said that the state had failed to show a convincing argument for barring same-sex marriages. He ordered the state to begin issuing marriage licenses to same-sex couples. But he suspended the order when the state once again appealed the ruling to the state supreme court.[14]

In April 1997, the Hawaii state legislature passed the most extensive package of rights and benefits ever given to same-sex couples in the United States. However, a second bill passed by the state legislature put a constitutional amendment on the Hawaii state ballot in November 1998 to allow the legislature to reserve marriage to heterosexual couples. Polls showed that in 1997, three fourths of the residents in Hawaii were opposed to same-sex marriages.[15]

Although other states are not required to follow the Hawaii decision, questions would come up if a gay couple married in Hawaii decided to move to another state. Under the full faith and credit clause of the United States Constitution (Article IV, Section 1), other states would be required to recognize same-sex marriages legally performed in Hawaii.[16]

Until 1996, the United States government accepted each state's definition of marriage. There was no federal law defining marriage. In 1996, the Defense of Marriage Act was passed by Congress and signed into law by President Bill Clinton. The law defines marriage in federal law as a union between one man and one woman.[17] Groups such as the American Civil Liberties Union strongly oppose the new law. They believe that it will deny homosexual couples rights enjoyed by heterosexual married couples. They also believe that it violates the constitutional guarantee of equal protection by making same-sex married couples second-class citizens.[18]

The Arguments Against Same-Sex Marriage

Much of the opposition to homosexual marriages comes from conservative Christians and orthodox Jews. They argue that marriage has been a necessary unit in civilization because it is the basis of the family. Permitting same-sex marriages would send society the message that traditional male-female marriages are not preferred. They believe that the government's responsibility is to encourage marriage and family stability.[19]

Those opposed to legalizing same-sex marriages believe that homosexuality is an immoral behavior that is forbidden in both the Old and New Testaments of the Bible. They say that legalizing marriage between two men or two women puts the stamp of respectability on what many consider sinful behavior and thus tears at the moral fiber of the country. Other people fear that changing the definition of marriage as a union between a man and a woman would open the door for legalizing unusual relationships, such as those between three or more people.[20]

Not all the objections come from heterosexuals. Some homosexuals question whether gay marriages will help gays and lesbians. They believe that rather than copying heterosexuals, they should work to make society accept their differences. They say that although gays and lesbians should have a right to marry, this is not a major goal. Gay liberation should focus on developing gay identity and on accepting many different kinds of relationships.[21]

The Arguments in Favor of Same-Sex Marriage

Those who fight to legalize same-sex marriages believe that the main issue is constitutional rather than religious. They point to the principles of individual liberty and equal protection before the law. Gays and lesbians have the same reasons for getting married that other people do. They want to gain the moral, legal, social, and spiritual benefits society gives to married couples and families.

Rock star Melissa Etheridge says, "I do believe that as an American citizen, a law-abiding, taxpaying—major—taxpaying citizen, that I should be allowed the same rights, the same pursuit of happiness that every other citizen enjoys. . . . As long as we have the same legal benefits and protections for me, and for my family—my family. That's all."[22]

The Human Rights Campaign, one of the nation's largest organizations fighting for gay and lesbian rights, says that marriage is a basic human right and a matter of personal decision. Government should not interfere in an individual's decision about whom to marry. They also point out that in the past people of different races were forbidden to marry for many of the same reasons given for banning same-sex marriages.[23]

Some polls show that the American public is uncertain about same-sex marriages. They worry about the long-term effects that such marriages might have on society. Many are afraid to express their hesitation because they don't want to be labeled prejudiced. Approximately 70 percent of Americans tell their politicians that they support most forms of gay rights, but they have reservations about same-sex marriages. A June 1996 survey in California by the Field Poll found that 57 percent of Californians opposed same-sex marriages. Many people tolerate homosexuality, but they don't want to approve of it.

Gays and Parental Rights

Central to the issue of parental rights is the question whether children are harmed when they are raised in a gay environment. It is estimated that there are somewhere between 6 million and 14 million gay and lesbian parents in the United States. Because many gay parents conceal their sexual orientations out of fear of losing their children in custody battles, the number of families headed by homosexuals is unknown. Some of these parents had children through alternative means of conception or through adoption. Others have custody of children who were born while they were in traditional marriages.

In 1991, it was estimated that there were five thousand gay households with children in San Francisco. Statistics from fertility clinics in large cities show that a significant number of lesbian women have received artificial insemination.[24]

Some gay men seek to become fathers with the help of a surrogate mother. The woman is artificially inseminated with the man's sperm and becomes pregnant. After she gives birth to the baby, the custody goes to the man. The process is very expensive. In 1991, the surrogate process cost approximately thirty-five thousand dollars for each child.[25]

A survey by the American Psychological Association of more than forty research projects on gay parenting found that children of gay parents were as likely to be well-adjusted as children raised in more traditional situations. They were no more likely to be homosexual than were children raised in a conventional family. Alex, an Oregon teenager with two lesbian moms, is an honor student: "Not to brag or anything, but if you compared me with an average kid in a normal household, I probably get better grades; I'm probably more athletic. I'm probably equally mentally healthy."[26]

Problems for Children of Same-Sex Parents

Some children of homosexual parents do have special problems. Some are ashamed to tell their friends that their parents are gay because they are afraid of the prejudice of their classmates. Kate, a teenager in Connecticut, was harassed by classmates who wrote "Kate's a Lesbo. Your Mom's Recruit" on her school locker.[27]

Not everyone agrees that gays make good parents and create stable family relationships. "Being gay should never result in being harassed, hated or hurt. But sadly, being gay also should never mean being able to marry or adopt. Everything in life has a price.

Being childless is a high price. But a child's basic needs must always supersede the desires of an adult," says Susan Carpenter McMillan, spokesperson for the Pasadena, California-based Woman's Coalition.[28]

In many instances, gays and lesbians have had their children taken from them. Sharon Bottoms, a lesbian in Virginia, lost the custody of her son to her mother. After Bottoms and her husband divorced, she moved in with her lover. Bottoms's mother was offended by her daughter's lesbianism. Although an appeals court had ruled that homosexuality alone was not sufficient grounds for losing custody of a child, the state supreme court ruled four to three that Bottoms should not have custody because lesbianism could prejudice others against the child.[29]

Gays argue that many children raised by heterosexual parents also have problems. They point to many studies indicating that children of gay and lesbian parents are well adjusted. In his court decision in the Hawaiian case ordering the state to issue marriage licenses to same-sex couples, Judge Chang wrote that the most important thing in raising happy, healthy children is the caring relationship between parent and child.[30]

7

Health Care Equality and the AIDS Epidemic

On the morning of October 2, 1985, when news of the death of actor Rock Hudson was reported, public awareness became newly focused on Acquired Immunodeficiency Syndrome (AIDS). The syndrome renders victims extremely vulnerable to life-threatening diseases such as hepatitis, tuberculosis, rare forms of skin and brain cancers, and a rare form of pneumonia. Researchers discovered that AIDS is caused by Human Immunodeficiency Virus (HIV). Reports that gay men and drug users who shared needles were being diagnosed with a rare new disease had appeared in the news media since the late 1970s. But many people had ignored the reports because they thought that the disease struck only homosexuals and people from other countries. By 1985, approximately twelve thousand Americans had died or were dying of AIDS. Not all the cases were drug users and homosexuals.[1] Other cases involved heterosexuals who had sex with an infected partner, children who contracted HIV from their mothers before, during, or after birth (due to breast feeding), and people who had transfusions of blood contaminated with the virus.[2]

The AIDS Death Toll

By June 1997, the death toll from AIDS in the United States had risen to 379,258. Approximately 612,078 people had been diagnosed with the disease.[3] Many of those who had died were gay men.

In the early 1980s, many people's response to the AIDS epidemic was fear, panic, and homophobia. Many homosexuals were treated with prejudice, and people who were infected with the virus found that they were discriminated against on the job, in finding housing, and in seeking health care. Some health professionals feared treating them, and a number of insurance companies refused to insure any homosexual male. In 1983, in San Jose, California, two nurses quit their jobs rather than treat an AIDS patient. The New York State Funeral Directors Association recommended that members refuse to embalm people who died from the disease.[4] Many

The Names Project Foundation encourages safe sex practices. The Names Quilt, made up of blocks of fabric honoring individuals who have died from AIDS, was displayed in its entirety in Washington, D.C., in 1996.

AIDS victims were uninsured or underinsured for the illness and had to seek help from public services. Those who were unable to continue working lost their health insurance benefits.[5]

Conservative religious and political organizations fanned the anxieties. In 1983, the pro-family Christian Coalition organized opposition to the National Gay Rodeo in Reno, Nevada, stating that those in attendance would spread AIDS throughout Nevada. A leader of the Moral Majority, a conservative religious organization, was quoted by gay author Randy Shilts in his book about the history of the AIDS epidemic, *And the Band Played On*. The man said, "We feel the deepest sympathy for AIDS victims, but I'm upset that the government is not spending more money to protect the general public from the gay plague." Another Moral Majority spokesman warned, "If homosexuals are not stopped, they will in time infect the entire nation, and America will be destroyed."[6]

In response, the attention and energy of the gay community became focused on demanding fair health care and treatment of people suffering from the illness. Groups such as the New York–based Gay Men's Health Crisis worked to help individuals, both homosexual and heterosexual, who were infected with the virus. In 1982, Southern California activists founded AIDS Project Los Angeles to educate the community to prevent the spread of the disease. Among the programs started by the organization were a food pantry for AIDS patients, a dental treatment center, and a buddy program that trained volunteers to provide one-to-one social interaction and emotional support for people with AIDS.[7]

Groups such as the American Civil Liberties Union, an organization that is concerned with protecting the constitutional rights of individuals, worried that the AIDS crisis was being used as an excuse for prejudice against those who were suffering from the illness.[8] People with AIDS were often denied access to employment, housing, schools, and health care because of unjustified fears about the disease.

Testing Controversy

The government and many health care professionals wanted to find a way to test blood for the virus that causes AIDS. In early 1985, Abbott Laboratories introduced the first AIDS antibody test in San Francisco. The test was to be used on donated blood to protect the blood supply. Little plastic beads were coated with the AIDS virus and then exposed to samples of donated blood. If a drop of infected blood was placed on the bead, the antibodies in the blood sample would attach themselves to the virus. After the bead was washed with various dyes and chemicals it would turn purple if antibodies were present, indicating that the blood sample contained the virus.[9]

Many gay activists were opposed to widespread testing, which they feared might lead to increased discrimination. They believed the tests violated the privacy of AIDS victims. Some of the anxiety also came from suggestions that public health officials might keep lists of those who tested positive. There was fear that the information could be used against gay men and women in the more than twenty states where homosexuality was illegal. There was also fear that some employers and insurance companies might require applicants to take the test. The diagnosis of AIDS could mean the loss of a job, housing, and health care. Forty-eight hours after the Abbott Laboratories test was licensed, the National Gay Task Force and the Lambda Legal Defense and Education Fund filed petitions with the federal court to stop the licensing of the test until more was known about its accuracy.

The concerns of the gay rights activists had a basis in truth. In some communities, fear of AIDS resulted in hysteria. A state health officer from Florida was contacted by a school district that wanted to weed out gay teachers and by a country club that wanted to test food workers. Although the AIDS virus is not airborne, some people suggested that individuals with the AIDS virus should be isolated and quarantined so that they couldn't infect others.

AIDS Testing Implemented

In California, the state legislature passed a law governing how the test could be given. No one would be forced to take the test without their written consent, and employers and insurers could not require applicants to take the test. The results were to be confidential. Because some people became suicidal after finding out that they had the illness, the law required psychological counseling.

In New York City, gay leaders strongly opposed AIDS testing because they were afraid that the rights of homosexuals might be violated. The health commissioner issued a rule that the test would not be permitted except for research. Many people, including gays, opposed this policy. They pointed out that some people wanted to take the test so that they could begin treatments if they tested positive. Also, some women who were drug users wanted to know if they were infected before they decided to have children.

Other states began to follow California's policy. They were encouraged by Senator Orrin Hatch of Utah. Hatch, a conservative, believed that the testing was necessary for public health. But he also knew that gay men would not want to be tested if the results were not confidential.[10]

Public health authorities worried that infected blood might expose people in need of transfusions to the HIV virus. In 1985, the United States Public Health Service established a policy stating that blood donors would be told their blood would be screened for the virus. If they tested positive, they would be

Act Up is an activist organization that fights for laws to provide health care for those suffering from AIDS.

told privately and their names would be placed on a list of unacceptable donors.[11]

Public panic about the AIDS epidemic continued. In California, the American Civil Liberties Union challenged a proposition on the state ballot in November 1986. The proposition asked voters to approve amendments to the state's health and safety code that would define AIDS as an infectious, contagious disease. The amendments would have then required the state to enforce the code against carriers of the disease. The ACLU believed that if passed, the proposition would violate the civil liberties of people suffering from AIDS. They argued that children with the virus might be forbidden to attend school. Funerals of those who died from AIDS-related illnesses might also be forbidden. The names of infected individuals and even those suspected of being HIV carriers would have to be reported to health departments. The ballot proposal was defeated by voters at the election.[12]

Supporters of Mandatory Testing

Former United States congressman William Dannemeyer is an outspoken backer of testing for the AIDS virus. In his book *Shadow in the Land*, he argues that early detection leads to more effective treatment. He also believes that determining who carries the virus will help stop the disease because these persons can be educated to avoid exposing others. Testing would also help determine how many Americans have been infected.

Dannemeyer is in favor of a national policy of reporting HIV infection. In the past, he argues, cases of other sexually transmitted diseases such as syphilis and gonorrhea were reported, which helped control the spread of new infections. Mandatory reporting would help authorities identify infected people to get them started on treatment. The reporting could be confidential, although there should also be an effort to notify sexual partners of an infected person that they may have been exposed to the virus.[13]

Everyone agrees that AIDS is a serious illness and health care issue. AIDS activists continue to fight for the personal freedoms of those who are infected with the virus. They believe that education about safe sex will do much to keep people from contracting the illness. Other people continue to voice their concern about the illness as a public health problem. They wonder if those with AIDS should be identified and possibly confined so that they won't spread the disease to others.

In 1998, the Gay Men's Health Crisis changed its policy of opposition to testing. It decided to support plans to report HIV-positive people to the New York State Health Department, using coded information rather than names to identify infected individuals. GMHC believes that a new kind of monitoring system is needed to help provide early treatment programs for HIV-infected individuals who do not have full-blown AIDS symptoms. The organization also favors continuing free, publicly funded anonymous testing.[14]

In the 1990s, AIDS infection increased among heterosexual men and women in the United States. Worldwide, more than 70 percent of adult HIV infections occur through heterosexual transmission.[15] But new treatments for the disease have begun to offer some hope. Prejudice against those who have the virus is less than it was in the 1980s, thanks in part to the battles fought by the gay community and their supporters to change public opinion. More people began to realize that AIDS is not a gay disease but an illness that can infect anyone.

Lesbians' Health Issues

Lesbians as a group have one of the lowest rates of infection with the AIDS virus. Nevertheless, like gay men, they have experienced problems when seeking health care. The National Gay and Lesbian Task Force has gathered many case histories of discrimination against lesbians by the health care industry.

Some women are unable to get health insurance. Because Marcia was unemployed she did not have health insurance. Her partner of eight years was unable to include Marcia on her health insurance policy. When Marcia discovered a lump in her breast, she could not get treatment.[16]

Other problems arise when a woman is hospitalized. After Sonja had breast cancer surgery, the hospital staff would not allow her partner to visit her in the recovery room, although other members of the family were escorted in by the nurses. The partner was afraid to complain because she feared health workers might treat Sonja badly.[17]

Many lesbians try to hide their sexual orientation from medical professionals because they have found that some health professionals are insensitive and prejudiced against homosexuals. In one example cited by the National Gay and Lesbian Task Force, a woman named Fran was roughly treated in an exam after she told her doctor she was a lesbian. "I'm just trying to change your mind," he said.[18]

Lack of considerate treatment from health professionals has led many lesbians to put off receiving medical care for as long as possible. Statistics from the National Cancer Institute show that 45 percent of lesbian women do not receive regular care from gynecologists (specialists in women's reproductive health). Studies show that these women are at high risk from breast cancer and cancers of the reproductive organs, diseases that many times can be successfully treated if they are discovered early.[19]

Although doctors need a patient's complete medical history to provide good care, many lesbians have been afraid to tell their physicians about their sexual orientation. In one study, 38 percent of lesbian women said they believed that telling a doctor or a nurse of their sexual orientation would result in their receiving poor health care. There is reason for their fears. A study in 1991 found that more than 50 percent of nursing students were prejudiced against lesbians; 15 percent of the students thought that lesbians' sexual behavior should be illegal.[20]

Many lesbians also feel that their community has been overlooked in the AIDS crisis. Many researchers presume that lesbians are not at great risk for this illness, but some studies have shown that over 30 percent of women with HIV symptoms have had sexual relations with other women. Some of these women have acquired the disease because they are intravenous drug users. One woman, a mother of three, said, "I'm a gay woman, living with AIDS. Nobody out here believes I'm real."[21]

Concerns of Lesbians with AIDS

In 1993, a group of HIV-positive lesbians, activists, and health officials met with Secretary of Health and Human Services Donna Shalala in Washington, D.C. The comments of the women who had AIDS showed their fears about the health system and the need for better medical treatment aimed at lesbians.

One woman had dropped out of a drug treatment and support group for HIV-positive women because she was afraid to admit that she was a lesbian. She said, "I stopped going to that place (drug treatment) because I didn't know what they would say in the group when I started talking about my (female) lover." Another said, "There's no category for lesbian women with HIV. Like we don't exist. Nobody's looking at lesbian couples with one HIV-positive and one HIV-negative to see if the virus is passed. It's like our lives don't matter."[22]

8

Should Gay Civil Rights Be Protected by Law?

Many gays and lesbians believe that there is a need for civil rights laws to protect homosexuals as a minority group. Although some states and cities have such laws, gay activists would like to see national legislation specifically guaranteeing homosexuals equal treatment.

Gay activists would like to see sexual orientation added to the list of protected categories in civil rights legislation so that discrimination against homosexuals would be illegal throughout the United States. These activists believe that homosexuality is a characteristic that a person cannot change, similar to a person's race or gender. It is illegal to discriminate because of a person's race or gender. Gays believe that they do not receive equal treatment because discrimination against homosexuals is not against the law in many parts of the United States.

As of 1998, there were two federal hate crime laws that address crimes against gays and lesbians. The Hate Crime Statistics Act, which was passed in 1990, calls for states and communities to report all hate crimes to the Federal Bureau of Investigation, although the law does not punish hate crimes. The Hate Crime Sentencing Enhancement Act provides for tougher sentencing for proven hate crimes. The law can only be used if the offense occurs on federal property.[1]

Bowers v. *Hardwick* and Privacy

In 1986, a Supreme Court ruling in the case of *Bowers* v. *Hardwick* established that the right to privacy did not cover homosexual activity. The right to privacy or the right to be left alone is not specifically stated in the United States Constitution, but it has been upheld through interpretation of the Fourth, Fifth, Ninth, and Fourteenth Amendments to the Constitution. The Fourth Amendment guarantees the right of people to be secure in their homes against unreasonable searches and seizures. The Fifth Amendment guarantees that a person's liberty cannot be taken without due process of law. The Ninth Amendment states that even though certain rights are stated in the Constitution, it cannot be interpreted in a way that denies other rights kept by the people. The Fourteenth Amendment states that no one can be denied equal protection of the law. The right to privacy has also been supported by a series of Supreme Court decisions. These include the 1967 landmark case *Loving* v. *Virginia*, which made interracial marriage legal.[2]

Michael Hardwick is a gay man who was arrested and charged with sodomy in the state of Georgia. He was arrested when his roommate allowed the police to come into their house to serve a traffic warrant. The police entered Hardwick's bedroom and found him in bed with another man. Hardwick was convicted of the charge of sodomy.

Hardwick and his attorneys argued that the Georgia law against sodomy violated his right to privacy. The federal court of appeals agreed with Hardwick's argument and ruled that Georgia's sodomy law was unconstitutional. The appeals court stated that he had engaged in a private act with a consenting adult.[3]

The state of Georgia appealed to the United States Supreme Court. In a five-to-four decision the justices reversed the opinion of the court of appeals and ruled that Georgia's sodomy law was legal. In the majority decision, written by Supreme Court Justice Byron White, the court said that the Constitution did not protect same-sex activity even when it occurred between consenting adults in the privacy of one's home. White wrote that sodomy is not a fundamental right protected by the Constitution. To support this decision, Chief Justice Warren Burger said sodomy laws were necessary because they were rooted in Jewish and Christian moral standards. This decision left it up to each state to determine whether or not sodomy would be considered illegal.

Four supreme court justices disagreed with the majority opinion. In his dissenting opinion, Justice Harry Blackmun stated that depriving individuals of the right to choose how they would live their lives posed a threat to the Constitution and to American values.[4] He wrote, "What the Court really has refused to recognize is the fundamental interest all individuals have in controlling the nature of their intimate associations with others."[5]

The American Civil Liberties Union states that sodomy laws violate one of the sexual areas of privacy defined by the Supreme Court in a 1965 ruling. In that case, *Griswold* v. *Connecticut*, the court struck down a state law that forbade married couples from buying contraceptives. The court said that there are "zones of privacy" into which the government cannot interfere.

Are Gay Civil Rights Laws Necessary?

Conservative and religious groups such as the Traditional Values Coalition and the Family Research Council argue that a federal law forbidding discrimination against homosexuals is unnecessary. They believe that the rights of gays and lesbians are already guaranteed by the same laws that protect all Americans, including the Bill of Rights and federal and state laws. They argue against the claim that homosexuals are an abused minority.

Some conservatives argue that homosexuals already have a high level of political power. As examples, they point to political action committees such as the Human Rights Campaign Fund, which makes large donations to political candidates. Other critics say that gays want rights that heterosexuals do not have, such as the right to exhibit their sexual preference even if this offends others in the community. They believe that gays should keep their sexual preference hidden.[6]

Writer and radio commentator Dennis Prager says that gay activists want people to look at homosexuals as a persecuted minority. He argues,

Groups such as the Traditional Values Coalition and the Family Research Council fear that gay and lesbian rights will deteriorate family and religious values.

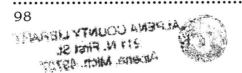

however, that they are not a minority in the same way that African Americans have been. While blacks have been discriminated against for who they are, homosexuals have been discriminated against for what they do. He believes that homosexuals should be treated decently and humanely, but he does not believe that society should be required to accept homosexuality as morally equal to heterosexuality. Passing laws to allow homosexuals to marry, for example, would send the message that the two lifestyles are equivalent.[7]

Some social conservatives claim that they are faced with a dilemma when it comes to discussing homosexuality. They believe that they are unfairly labeled as homophobic if they say they are against granting gays the right to get married or if they question whether gays should serve in the military. They believe that they should have a right to express their religious belief that homosexual practices are immoral. In a *Los Angeles Times* editorial, Elaine Minamide wrote, "To be categorized as homophobic hurts. Yet am I to turn my back on what I believe, compromise my convictions, invalidate what the Bible declares to be true, simply because a certain segment of society takes exception to my beliefs?"[8]

Some opponents of gay rights say that they have been unfairly harassed by individuals who disagree with their viewpoints. Marianne Moody Jennings, an Arizona columnist, wrote an article opposing same-sex marriages. Soon she began receiving hate mail and threats from people who disagreed with her. A three-inch screwdriver was jammed into a tire on her car. People wrote to Arizona State University, where she is employed as a teacher, demanding her dismissal. She and others believe they should have a right to voice their opinions even if they are unpopular with the gay community.[9]

Gay Rights Should Be Protected

In their book *Created Equal: Why Gay Rights Matter to America*, authors and gay rights advocates Michael Nava and Robert Dawidoff argue that the refusal of the courts to grant privacy rights and equal protection of the laws to gays and lesbians is based on prejudice. They say that even if the majority of people in the United States are heterosexual, the government has the obligation to protect the rights of the minority. They point out that gays and lesbians take part in society and support the country with their taxes. In America everybody deserves equal treatment by virtue of being a citizen. Denying the rights of one group means that any group can be discriminated against.[10]

In an editorial in the *Los Angeles Times*, Dawidoff argued for a broader discussion of sexual orientation and how it affects people's lives. He urged people to seriously discuss gay rights and the ways gays and lesbians could be integrated into American society. Such discussion is difficult, he said, because homosexuals are expected to debate those who regard homosexuality as a sin. Dawidoff wrote, "The time has come to include lesbians and

The Reverend Lou Sheldon, founder of the Traditional Values Coalition, is an outspoken opponent of legislation supporting gay and lesbian rights.

gays within the conversation about rights and obligations that define civil society."[11]

Other activists point to the high numbers of hate crimes against homosexuals as a reason for including homosexuals in the laws protecting minorities. According to a national study, antigay violence and victimization rose 31 percent in 1991. A Department of Justice study reported that homosexuals are probably the most frequent victims of hate crimes. There were 1,822 reported antigay incidents in five cities surveyed by the National Gay and Lesbian Task Force Policy Institute in 1991.[12]

The task force argues that homosexuals do not want special rights, just the same rights that belong to all American citizens. They say that the right to get and keep a job based on merit should be guaranteed to everyone. All should have the right to obtain housing, to stay in a hotel, and to be served in a restaurant. Being able to have and to raise one's children is a basic human desire. All people should be able to exist freely in society without fear of being attacked. Gay rights activists say that without civil rights laws that ban discrimination based on sexual orientation, gay men and lesbians could lose jobs, families, and homes, and be refused service in public places.[13]

Questions about gay and lesbian rights will continue to challenge Americans in the years to come. Should gays and lesbians serve openly in the military? Should they be able to legally marry and have equal rights in child custody? Should they be allowed to adopt children? Should gay students be allowed to have special school clubs and be able to participate openly in all school activities such as student government and dances? Should gays be treated equally on the job when it comes to hiring and promotion? What do you think about these timely issues?

Chapter Notes

Chapter 1. The Fight for Gay Rights

1. Gregory M. Herek and Kevin T. Berrill, eds., *Hate Crimes: Confronting Violence Against Lesbians and Gay Men* (Newbury Park, Calif.: Sage Publications, 1992), pp. 11–15.

2. Ibid., pp. 144–146.

3. James W. Button, Barbara A. Rienzo, and Kenneth D. Wald, *Private Lives, Public Conflicts: Battles over Gay Rights in American Communities* (Washington, D.C.: CQ Press, 1997), p. 60.

4. Michael Nava and Robert Dawidoff, *Created Equal: Why Gay Rights Matter to America* (New York: St. Martin's Press, 1995), pp. ix–xi.

5. Telephone interview with Mark Johnson, media director, National Gay and Lesbian Task Force, January 30, 1998.

6. Warren J. Blumenfeld and Diane Raymond, *Looking at Gay and Lesbian Life* (New York: Philosophical Library, 1988), p. 75.

7. Franz J. Kallmann, M.D., "Comparative Twin Study on the Genetic Aspects of Male Homosexuality," in Geoff Puterbaugh, ed., *Twins and Homosexuality: A Casebook* (New York: Garland Publishing, Inc., 1990), pp. 115–116.

8. Wayne S. Wooden and Jay Parker, *Men Behind Bars: Sexual Exploitation in Prison* (New York: Plenum Press, 1982), pp. 5, 15.

Chapter 2. The History of Homosexuality in Society

1. Warren J. Blumenfeld and Diane Raymond, *Looking at Gay and Lesbian Life* (New York: Philosophical Library, 1988), pp. 156–161.

2. Ibid., pp. 164–166.

3. Ibid., p. 199.

4. Ibid., pp. 199–200.

5. Michael George Scofield, *Society and the Homosexual* (New York: E. P. Dutton and Co, 1953), p. 80.

6. Judd Marmor, *Homosexual Behavior: A Modern Reappraisal* (New York: Basic Books, 1980), p. 93.

7. Jonathan N. Katz, *Gay American History: Lesbians and Gay Men in the U.S.A.* (New York: Meridian, 1992), p. 13.

8. Ibid., p. 12.

9. John Scagliotti, producer, *Before Stonewall: The Making of a Gay and Lesbian Community* (video), (Cinema Guild, 1984).

10. Katz, ibid., pp. 399–401.

11. Scagliotti, ibid.

12. Ibid.

13. Katz, ibid., pp. 385–392.

14. Ibid., pp. 412–413.

15. Ibid., pp. 415–416.

16. Judith C. Galas, *Gay Rights* (San Diego: Lucent Books, 1996), p. 20.

17. Scagliotti, ibid.

18. Ibid.

19. Blumenfeld and Raymond, ibid., p. 77.

20. Elaine Landau, *Different Drummer: Homosexuality in America* (New York: Julian Messner, 1986), pp. 46–49.

21. Ibid.

22. Ibid., pp. 52–55.

23. Scagliotti, ibid.

24. Ibid.

25. Galas, ibid., p. 28.

26. Blumenfeld and Raymond, ibid., p. 311.

27. Galas, ibid., pp. 28–30.

28. Randy Shilts, *And the Band Played On* (New York: St. Martin's Press, 1987), pp. 16–17.

Chapter 3. Discrimination on the Job

1. Bettina Boxall, "A Painful Lesson for a Gay Teacher," *Los Angeles Times*, June 18, 1995, pp. A1, 31.

2. Ibid.

3. Brian McNaught, *Gay Issues in the Workplace* (New York: St. Martin's Press, 1993), p. 2.

4. Lee Badgett, Colleen Donnelly, and Jennifer Kibbe, "Pervasive Patterns of Discrimination Against Lesbians and Gay Men: Evidence from Surveys Across the United States," National Gay and Lesbian Task Force, Washington, D.C., 1992, pp. 1–2, 4.

5. Warren J. Blumenfeld and Diane Raymond, *Looking at Gay and Lesbian Life* (New York: Philosophical Library, 1988), pp. 296–297.

6. Louise Sloan, "Do Ask, Do Tell: Lesbians Come Out at Work," *Glamour*, vol. 92, May 1994, pp. 242–243.

7. Ibid.

8. Bettina Boxall, "Scouts Can Bar Gay Men as Leaders, State Court Rules," *Los Angeles Times*, May 31, 1994, pp. A3, 23.

9. Personal interview with Jon Davidson, supervising attorney, Lambda Legal Defense and Education Fund, Western Regional Office, January 28, 1998.

10. Tom Perry, "State Court Upholds Firing of Gay Scout Leader," *Los Angeles Times*, May 23, 1997, pp. A3, 26.

11. Susan Salter Reynolds, "Gay, Lesbian Synagogue Celebrates 25th Year," *Los Angeles Times*, November 1, 1997, p. B4.

12. James W. Button, Barbara A. Rienzo, and Kenneth D. Wald, *Private Lives, Public Conflicts: Battles over Gay Rights in American Communities* (Washington, D.C.: CQ Press, 1997), pp. 27, 76.

13. Jack Nichols, *The Gay Agenda* (Amherst, N.Y.: Prometheus Books, 1996), p. 63.

14. Button, Rienzo, and Wald, ibid., p. 28.

15. Mark Thompson, ed., *Long Road to Freedom: The Advocate History of the Gay and Lesbian Movement* (New York: St. Martin's Press, 1994), p. 395.

16. Bettina Boxall, "Gay Rights Advocates Rejoice at Ruling," *Los Angeles Times*, May 21, 1996, p. A14.

17. Jack Nichols, ibid.

18. Mark Thompson, ibid., pp. 396–397.

19. *Hate on the Ballot* (video), issue 4, (Las Vegas: Network Qu., 1992).

20. Brian McNaught, *Homophobia in the Workplace* (video), (Motivational Media, 1993).

21. "Who Supports the Lesbian and Gay Rights Movement?" National Gay and Lesbian Task Force, Washington, D.C., n.d., pp. 1–2.

22. David W. Dunlap, "After Pressure from Activists, Congressman Admits Being Gay," *Los Angeles Daily News*, August 3, 1996, p. 18.

Chapter 4. Lesbian and Gay Issues at School

1. "Project 10, Summer Update," Fairfax High School, Los Angeles, 1996, p. 1.

2. Ibid., p. 2.

3. Diane Klein, "When Hand Holding's a Threat," *Los Angeles Times*, May 3, 1993, p. E4.

4. Mark Walsh, "Gay-Rights Ruling Seen Holding Wide Implications for Education," *Education Week*, March 29, 1996, p. 1.

5. Mark Walsh, "Gay Students' Request Spurs Board to Cut Clubs," *Education Week*, February 26, 1996, p. 6.

6. Jeff Archer, "Equal Access of Law at Center of Utah Flap," *Education Week*, March 6, 1996, pp. 1, 13.

7. Ibid.

8. Jeff Archer, "Firestorm in Wake of Salt Lake City Vote Continues to Grow," *Education Week*, March 6, 1996, p. 12.

9. Ibid.

10. Brian McNaught, *Homophobia in the Workplace* (video), (Motivational Media, 1993).

11. Bruce Mirken, "School Programs Should Stress Acceptance of Homosexuality," in William Dudley, ed., *Homosexuality: Opposing Viewpoints* (San Diego: Greenhaven Press, 1993), p. 108. Reprinted from "Gay Teens," *Genre*, 1992.

12. "Debunking the Myth of Gay Youth Suicide," Policy Concerns, Concerned Women for America, 1996, pp. 1–2.

13. Michael Quintanilla, "No Other Place to Go," in Dudley, ibid., p. 111. Reprinted from *Los Angeles Times*, December 7, 1989.

14. Mirken, ibid., pp. 109–112.

15. Ibid., p. 110.

16. Patricia Smith, "School Programs Should Not Stress Acceptance of Homosexuality," in Dudley, ibid., p. 113. Reprinted from "Project 10: Not What It Seems," *The Family*, November 1992.

17. Mark Walsh, "Gay Students Press Abuse Claims Against District," *Education Week*, April 14, 1996, p. 5.

18. Clifford Rothman, "A Stand for Human Worth," *Los Angeles Times*, February 26, 1997, pp. E1, 6.

19. Rothman, ibid., p. E6.

20. Linda Jacobson, "Gay Student to Get Nearly $1 Million in Settlement," *Education Week*, November 27, 1996, p. 7.

Chapter 5. Gays and Lesbians in the Military

1. Randy Shilts, *Conduct Unbecoming: Gays and Lesbians in the U.S. Military* (New York: St. Martin's Press, 1993), p. 15.

2. Arthur Dong, director, *Coming Out Under Fire* (video), (Fox Lorber Associates, 1993).

3. Shilts, ibid., p. 203.

4. Ibid., pp. 208, 210, 212, 228, 239.

5. Ibid., pp. 248–264.

6. American Civil Liberties Union, "Lesbian and Gay Rights," *ACLU Briefing Paper*, no. 18, New York, n.d.

7. Shilts, ibid., pp. 264, 285–286.

8. Ibid., pp. 319–320, 362, 366.

9. Ibid., pp. 682–683.

10. John Balzar, "Lesbian Army Officer Wins Battle in Court," *Los Angeles Times*, June 2, 1994, pp. A3, 21.

11. American Civil Liberties Union and Lambda Legal Defense and Education Fund, Inc., "Fact Sheet: *Able* v. *USA*," *American Civil Liberties Union*, n.d., <http://www.aclu.org/news/n070297c.html>.

12. Craig Donegan, "The 'Don't Ask, Don't Tell' Ban: An Overview," in Tamara L. Roleff, ed., *Gay Rights* (San Diego: Greenhaven Press, 1997), pp. 91–93. Reprinted from "New Military Culture," *CQ Researcher*, April 26, 1996.

13. "Expanded Coverage: The Fourth Annual Report on 'Don't Ask, Don't Tell, Don't Pursue,'" *Servicemembers Legal Defense Network page*, February 19, 1993, <http://www.sldn.org/reports/fourth.htm> (April 28, 1998).

14. David Hackworth, "The Military Should Not Accept Homosexuals," in William Dudley, ed., *Homosexuality: Opposing Viewpoints* (San Diego: Greenhaven Press, 1993), pp. 102–104. Reprinted from "A Voice from the Trenches Says Keep Gays Out of the Military," *The Washington Post National Weekly Edition*, July 6–12, 1992.

15. Eric Konigsberg, "The Military Should Accept Homosexuals," in Dudley, ibid., pp. 96–99. Reprinted from "Gays in Arms," *The Washington Monthly*, November 1992.

16. "Sexual Orientation and U.S. Military Personnel Policy: Options and Assessment," *The Real News page*, n.d., <http://www.rain.org/~open mind/randgays.html>.

17. Ryan J. Lepicier, "Gays in the Military," n.d., <http://gladstone.uoregon.edu/~ryan/military. htm>.

18. American Civil Liberties Union and Lambda Legal Defense and Education Fund, ibid.

19. "For the First Time, NY Federal Judge Strikes Down Entire Law Barring Gays from Military Service," *Lambda Legal Defense and Education Fund Press Release*, August 2, 1997, <http://www. Lambdalegal.org/cgi-bin/pages/documents/ record?record=73>.

20. Ibid.

Chapter 6. Same-Sex Marriage and Gay Parents

1. Barbara Kantrowitz, "Gay Families Come Out," *Newsweek*, November 4, 1996, pp. 51–56.

2. Ibid., pp. 51–52.

3. Mark Miller, "We're a Family and We Have Rights," *Newsweek*, November 4, 1996, pp. 54–55.

4. Richard Stengel, "For Better or For Worse?" *Time*, June 3, 1996, pp. 52–53. "Lesbian and Gay Family Fact Sheet," National Gay and Lesbian Task Force Policy Institute, Washington, D.C., May 1995, pp. 1–2.

5. Elizabeth Birch, "A Basic Human Right: Talking About Gay Marriage," *Human Rights Campaign*, n.d., <http://www.hrc.org./issues/ marriage/guide.html>.

6. Ibid., p. 3.

7. Stengel, ibid., p. 52.

8. "ACLU Background Briefing: Congress Considers Anti-Gay Marriage Bill and Employment Non-Discrimination Act," *American Civil Liberties Union*, n.d., <http://www.aclu.org/issues/gay/endaback.html>, p. 3.

9. "Lesbian and Gay Family Fact Sheet," ibid.

10. Eadie Gieb, "LAUSD Needn't Give Benefits to Same-Sex Partners," *Los Angeles Daily News*, January 20, 1997, p. A19.

11. Mary N. Cameli, "Gay and Lesbian Partners Should Be Legally Recognized as Family Members," in Tamara L. Roleff, ed., *Gay Rights* (San Diego: Greenhaven Press, 1997), pp. 30–34. Reprinted from "Extending Family Benefits to Gay Men and Lesbian Women," *Chicago-Kent Law Review*, vol. 68, no. 1, 1992, p. 447.

12. "Domestic Partnership Benefits for Same-Sex Couples," *Human Rights Campaign*, n.d., <http://www.hrc.org/issues/workplace/dp/index.html>.

13. Susan Essoyan and Bettina Boxall, "Hawaii Ruling Lifts Ban on Marriage of Same-Sex Couples," *Los Angeles Times*, December 4, 1996, pp. A1, 17.

14. "Same-Sex Marriage: Where the Issue Stands," *Human Rights Campaign*, n.d., <http://www.hrc.org/issues/marriage/marria.html>.

15. Susan Essoyan, "Hawaii Approves Benefits Package for Gay Couples," *Los Angeles Times*, April 30, 1997, pp. A3, 14.

16. "Same-Sex Marriage: Where the Issue Stands," ibid.

17. "Clinton Becomes First President to Intrude on States' Jurisdiction over Marriage," *Human Rights Campaign*, n.d., <http://www.hrc.org/issues/marriage/index x 002.html>.

18. "ACLU Background Briefing," ibid.

19. Bruce Fein and Dinesh D'Souza, "Society Should Not Sanction Gay Partnerships," in William Dudley, ed., *Homosexuality: Opposing Viewpoints* (San Diego: Greenhaven Press, 1993), pp. 169–170. Reprinted from Bruce Fein, "No: Reserve Marriage for Heterosexuals," *ABA Journal*, January 1990; and Dinesh D'Souza, "From Tolerance to Subsidy," *Crisis*, September 1989.

20. "In Their Own Words: The Homosexual Activist Agenda for Marriage," *Alert*, Family Research Council, Washington, D.C., 1996, p. 1.

21. Paula L. Ettelbrick, "Legalizing Gay Marriage Would Harm Homosexuals," in Dudley, ibid., pp. 177–178. Reprinted from "Since When Is Marriage a Path to Liberation?" *Out/Look*, Fall 1989.

22. Kantrowitz, ibid., pp. 55.

23. Birch, ibid., pp. 4–5.

24. Scott Harris, "2 Moms or 2 Dads—and a Baby," *Los Angeles Times*, October 20, 1991, pp. A1, 16.

25. Ibid., p. 16.

26. Joseph P. Shapiro and Stephen Gregory, "Kids with Gay Parents," *U.S. News and World Report*, September 16, 1996, pp. 75–76.

27. Ibid., p. 79.

28. Susan Carpenter McMillan, "Do Gay Partners and Parents Have a Place in the Family of Values?" *Los Angeles Times*, December 26, 1996, p. B7.

29. "Lesbian Mother Abandons Fight to Get Son Back," *Los Angeles Times*, August 16, 1996, p. A24.

30. Carey Goldberg, A Victory for Same-Sex Parenting, at Least," *The New York Times*, December 5, 1996, p. A20.

Chapter 7. Health Care Equality
and the AIDS Epidemic

1. Randy Shilts, *And the Band Played On* (New York: St. Martin's Press, 1987), pp. xxi–xxiii.

2. "Why you should be informed about AIDS," (South Deerfield, Mass.: Channing L. Bete Co., 1984), pp. 6–7.

3. "Statistical Information on HIV/AIDS Cases," *Centers for Disease Control and Prevention National AIDS Clearinghouse*, n.d., <http://www.cdcnac.org/nastats.html> (April 23, 1998).

4. Shilts, ibid., p. 321.

5. Cindy Patton, "Civil Rights Must Take Priority in Controlling AIDS," in Tom Modl and Lynn Hall, eds., *AIDS: Opposing Viewpoints* (San Diego: Greenhaven Press, 1987), p. 105.

6. Shilts, ibid., p. 322.

7. "AIDS Project Los Angeles: A Historical Overview," AIDS Project Los Angeles, Winter 1998.

8. "HIV/AIDS," *American Civil Liberties Union*, n.d., <http://www.aclu.org/issues/aids/isaids.html>.

9. Shilts, ibid., p. 539.

10. Ibid., pp. 541–543.

11. Ronald Bayer, *Private Acts, Social Consequences: AIDS and the Politics of Public Health* (New York: Free Press, 1989), pp. 89–93.

12. Ibid., pp. 147–149.

13. William Dannemeyer, *Shadow in the Land: Homosexuality in America* (San Francisco: Ignatius Press, 1989), pp. 211–214.

14. "Facts and Statistics," *Gay Men's Health Crisis*, December 1, 1997, <http://www.gmhc.org/glance/facts.html>.

15. "Names Reporting," *ACT UP*, n.d., <http://www.Actupuny.org/alert/names01.html>.

16. Risa Denenberg, "Invisible Women, Lesbians and Health Care," in *Lesbian Health Care: Selected Articles* (Washington D.C.: National Gay and Lesbian Task Force Policy Institute, 1994), p. 4. Reprinted from *Health/PAC Bulletin*, Spring 1992.

17. Ibid., pp. 3–4.

18. Ibid., p. 4.

19. Victoria A. Brownworth, "The Other Epidemic, Lesbians and Breast Cancer," in *Lesbian Health Care*, ibid., p. 13. Reprinted from *OUT Magazine*, February/March 1993.

20. Nancy Warren, "Out of the Question," in *Lesbian Health Care*, ibid., p. 15. Reprinted from *SIECUS Report*, October/November 1993.

21. Ibid., p. 18.

22. Ibid.

Chapter 8. Should Gay Civil Rights Be Protected by Law?

1. "Fighting Anti-Gay Hate Crimes," Human *Rights Campaign*, n.d., <http://www.hrc.org/issues/hate.index.html>.

2. American Civil Liberties Union, "Lesbian and Gay Rights," *ACLU Briefing Paper*, no. 18, New York, n.d.

3. Michael Nava and Robert Dawidoff, *Created Equal: Why Gay Rights Matter to America* (New York: St. Martin's Press, 1995), p. 59.

4. Ibid., pp. 66–67.

5. American Civil Liberties Union, ibid.

6. "Homosexuality Is Not a Civil Right," *Family Research Council*, Washington, D.C., n.d., pp. 1–2.

7. Dennis Prager, "Biblical Roots of Right and Wrong," *Los Angeles Times*, July 16, 1993, p. B13.

8. Elaine Minamide, "Sticks and Stones and Homophobes," *Los Angeles Times*, July 16, 1993, p. B13.

9. Marianne Moody Jennings, "Same-Sex Marriage Critic Punished by Intolerance," *Arizona Republic*, July 28, 1996, p. H3.

10. Nava and Dawidoff, ibid., pp. 161–167.

11. Robert Dawidoff, "First, We Demand Recognition," *Los Angeles Times*, July 16, 1993, p. B13.

12. "Countering Right-Wing Rhetoric," *National Gay and Lesbian Task Force Policy Institute*, Washington, D.C., 1992, p. 1.

13. Ibid., p. 1–2.

Further Reading

Books

Cory, Donald Webster. *The Homosexual in America*. New York: Castle Books, 1951.

Dudley, William, ed. *Homosexuality: Opposing Viewpoints*. San Diego: Greenhaven Press, 1993.

Galas, Judith C. *Gay Rights*. San Diego: Lucent Books, 1996.

Landau, Elaine. *Different Drummer: Homosexuality in America*. New York: Julian Messner, 1986.

McNaught, Brian. *Gay Issues in the Workplace*. New York: St. Martin's Press, 1993.

Nava, Michael, and Robert Dawidoff. *Created Equal: Why Gay Rights Matter to America*. New York: St. Martin's Press, 1994.

Shilts, Randy. *And the Band Played On: Politics, People, and the AIDS Epidemic*. New York: St. Martin's Press, 1987.

———. *Conduct Unbecoming: Gays and Lesbians in the U.S. Military*. New York: St. Martin's Press, 1993.

Articles

Boxall, Bettina. "A Painful Lesson for a Gay Teacher." *Los Angeles Times*, June 18, 1995, pp. Al, 31.

Essoyan, Susan, and Bettina Boxall. "Hawaii Ruling Lifts Ban on Marriage of Same-Sex Couples." *Los Angeles Times*, December 4, 1996, pp. Al, 17.

Kantrowitz, Barbara. "Gay Families Come Out." *Newsweek*, November 4, 1996, pp. 51–56.

Sloan, Louise. "Do Ask, Do Tell: Lesbians Come Out at Work." *Glamour*, May 1994, pp. 242–243.

Williamson, Alistair D. "Is This the Right Time to Come Out?" *Harvard Business Review*, July–August 1993, pp. 18–2O.

Videos

Dong, Arthur, director. *Coming Out Under Fire*. Fox Lorber Associates, 1993.

Hate on the Ballot, issue 4. Las Vegas: Network Qu., 1992.

McNaught, Brian. *Homophobia in the Workplace*. Motivational Media, 1993.

Scagliotti, John, producer. *Before Stonewall: The Making of a Gay and Lesbian Community*. Cinema Guild, 1984.

Organizations Concerned with Gay Rights

American Civil Liberties Union (ACLU)
132 W. 43rd St.
New York, NY 10036
(212) 944-9800
The ACLU handles legal cases and helps make policy on behalf of gays.

Concerned Women for America
370 L'Enfant Promenade SW, Suite 800
Washington, DC 20024
(202) 488-0806
This organizations advocates traditional family values; it opposes gay marriages and the granting of additional rights to gays.

The Eagle Forum Education Center
7800 Bonhomme
St. Louis, MO 63105
(314) 721-1213
An advocacy group for the pro-family movement.

Equal Rights Marriage Fund (ERMF)
2001 M. St. NW
Washington, DC 20036
(202) 822-6546
Dedicated to the legalization of gay and lesbian marriage, ERMF serves as a national clearinghouse for gay and lesbian marriage rights.

Family Research Council
700 13th St. NW, Suite 500
Washington, DC 20005
(202) 393-2100
http://www.frc.org
The council provides research on the traditional family, defined as people connected by marriage, blood, or adoption. It opposes gay adoptions and marriages.

Focus on the Family
420 N. Cascade Ave.
Colorado Springs, CO 80910
This organization supports traditional family values and opposes homosexual marriage and adoption.

Friends of Project 10
7850 Melrose Ave.
Los Angeles, CA 90046
(213) 651-5200
Project 10 addresses the needs of gay, lesbian, and bisexual youths through programs in the school.

The Hetrick-Martin Institute
401 West St.
New York, NY 10014
(212) 633-8920
A nonprofit organization offering a range of social services to gay and lesbian teens and their families.

Lambda Legal Defense and Education Fund, Inc.
666 Broadway
New York, NY 10012
(212) 995-8585
The fund works to defend the rights of lesbians, gays, and people with HIV.

National Gay and Lesbian Task Force (NGLTF)
2320 17th St. NW
Washington, DC 20009-2702
(202) 322-6483
http://www.ngltf.org
NGLTF promotes rights for lesbians and gay men. It lobbies Congress and the White House on a full range of civil rights and AIDS issues, and it lobbies state legislatures to abolish sodomy laws.

Parents and Friends of Lesbians and Gays (PFLAG)
1101 14th St. NW, Suite 1030
Washington, DC 20005
(202) 638-4200
PFLAG provides support and education for gays, lesbians, bisexuals, and their families and friends. It works to end prejudice and discrimination against homosexuals and to protect and extend their civil rights.

Traditional Values Coalition

P.O. Box 940
Anaheim, CA 92815
(714) 520-0300
(202) 393-2100 Washington, DC

The coalition supports traditional family values. It strongly opposes same-sex marriages and adoptions.

Index

About the Author

Marilyn Tower Oliver is a former high school teacher turned journalist and writer. She has had more than two hundred articles published in regional and national publications. Books she has written for Enslow Publishers, Inc., include *Gangs: Trouble in the Streets*, *Drugs: Should They Be Legalized?*, *Prisons: Today's Debate*, and *Alcatraz Prison In American History*.